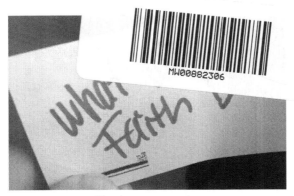


## Endorsements

"I love books—books of all types, but especially inspiring, "can't put it down" books like this one. *What Would Faith Do?* is a masterpiece of self-help full of autobiographical vulnerability and truth you'll want to remember and apply immediately. For spiritual seekers all over the world, read this to remember who you are. For anyone new to these ideas, be assured they're real and they work."

- Gayla Wick, Author of *The Character of True Intimacy: Finding the Love of Your Life.*

"One day, I was feeling really depleted, disconnected from passion and my love of life. I thought, *Okay, how can I get that back? How can I dwell within who I am meant to be and what I am really supposed to experience here*? I thought, *Well, duh, what would Faith do? I have Faith's book...so start reading it!* Reading about Faith's shift after her car accident (even though I had heard the story before) was exactly what I needed! I have struggled with an addiction to control and struggled with trusting in something greater. This book has been such a blessing in helping me grow and expand. Thank you, Faith, for sharing yourself with the world!"

- Cortni McBeth

"Through love and positivity, Faith Young has been able to overcome extraordinary challenges in her life. However, her story does not stop there. She serves as a living example of how any person in any circumstance can create love and abundance in their lives. Reading What Would Faith Do was a profound experience that gave me the tools to create more for my life--more strength, more abundance, more love and, of course, more Faith.

Five years ago at the height of my darkest days, I was blessed to meet a truly inspirational woman, Faith Young. During some of the greatest challenges in my life, not only did Faith support me, she gave me the tools to make positive changes that will impact my life profoundly and forever. I am truly honored to call her a mentor, coach and friend. She is a great example for all of us."

- Nichole Walker

# What Would Faith Do?

Alexandra,
You are Loved! allow yourself
to be Loved. You were meant
to shine. I believe in you!
I♡U

What Would Faith Do?
Create an Abundant Life Through "Faith"



Book Cover: Nick Zelinger
Editing: Donna Mazzitelli
Layout/Design: Andrea Costantine
Author Photograph: Mark Tempinski
UPSTREAM IMAGING

Printed in the United States of America
First Edition
ISBN 13: 978-1492746669

1. Self-Help 2. Manifesting

**Create an Abundant Life**
**Through “Faith"**

Faith Young

I dedicate this book to my friend, Maricela,
whose life has been an example
of love and abundance.

# Contents

# A Note to the Reader

Some of the stories revealed in the pages of this book actually happened to me. There are other stories that I witnessed directly. The final category of stories is made up of those that were disclosed to me through mutual friends or acquaintances. I have attempted to keep the accounts of all stories, including the circumstances and sequencing of events, as accurate as possible.

Every story and insight offered in *What Would Faith Do?* is shared with the intention to heal and inspire you, the reader, to know that no matter who you are, no matter where you live, and no matter what your current circumstances, I believe in you and all that is possible in your life. May you receive this book with the love and empowerment that I invite you to embrace.

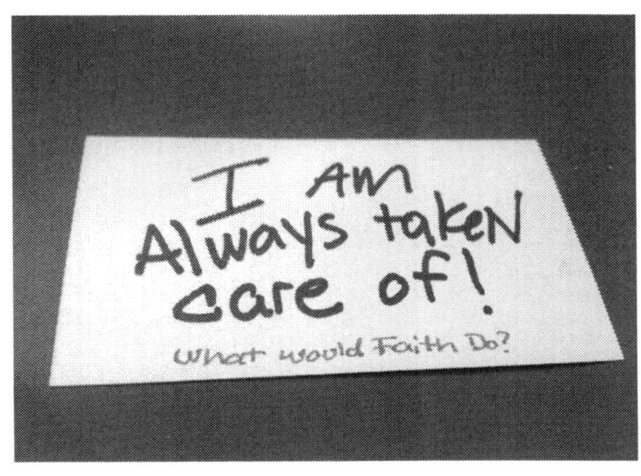


# Foreword

Written by Angel Tucey

It's no coincidence that my path crossed with Faith Young's. At a time when I was trying to create a movement of kindness on mainstream media, it was Faith who believed in my radio program more than anyone else. Faith invited me to her networking events and asked me to speak to her women's group about my experience and my vision for creating a nationally syndicated radio show. More than that, Faith linked arms with our cause and helped to spread the story to others. Daily, Faith would post her gratitude on our Facebook wall and call it a "Fan Brag."

When Faith asks how she can help, she acts on it. I don't believe in coincidence. I needed Faith in my life, and her belief and commitment planted the seed that is now almost four years old and gaining momentum. There's something positive on mainstream media? You betcha! *That's what Faith would do.*

I've watched firsthand as Faith Young created the 365 Days of Gratitude. Her acts of gratitude were the original common thread for us to use on the Experience Pros Radio Show. The world is full of anger and negativity, and media seems to enjoy spreading the bad news. There's more hurt and anger than ever, especially online where you can feel extremely disconnected from an actual human being. It seems commonplace to hear people criticize publically and then turn around and wonder what happened to kindness. Saying something nice to someone else takes courage. Sharing kind sentiments requires stepping out of scarcity and leaping into abundance and truly believing that every person and every little act of kindness is a gift.

Reading *What Would Faith Do*? filled my thoughts with energy that affirmed my belief in being positive. When you believe that anything is possible, people find their way to you and the coolest opportunities show up. Faith taught me to receive those gifts graciously, to say "thank you" to compliments, and to shower others with positive encouragement. My virtue is encouragement, and when Faith shows up on my Facebook wall with words of encouragement, I immediately recognize the perfect timing and make sure to pour love and gratitude onto someone else. Faith sprinkles positive magic fairy dust wherever she goes. I think it falls right out of her sparkly hair.

Faith's book reminds me that I am always taken care

of. I am so grateful to be receiving the love that Faith has put out into the world and to know that I am one of seven billion people who truly understand that our life is better because we remind ourselves every single day of our intentions, and that what we focus on we receive.

I've always been a goal-setter. I love writing down my goals and checking off my accomplishments. Looking back on the years, I'm excited to see what I've put my energy towards and what great things have come from that discipline. After reading Faith's book, however, I can see that in the past I allowed myself to be limited to creating those victories that I had already identified. I always had the mentality that "if were to be, it's up to me." I put a lot of time and attention on creating the "how." That's not my job. My job is to believe in the possibilities and the abundance that is out there for me, for my family, and for the one million (or more) future listeners.

Reading Faith's book is like taking a hot shower after a three-day camping trip. As you stand in the flow of hot water, you begin to feel lighter, as if you've lost weight, and every tense muscle relaxes as the grime flows down the drain. Stepping out into a clean, warm towel, you are relaxed and free to start again. *Right from where you are, brand new, like magic.*

- Angel Tuccy, co-host of The Experience Pros Radio Show, The Most Positive Business Talk Show in America

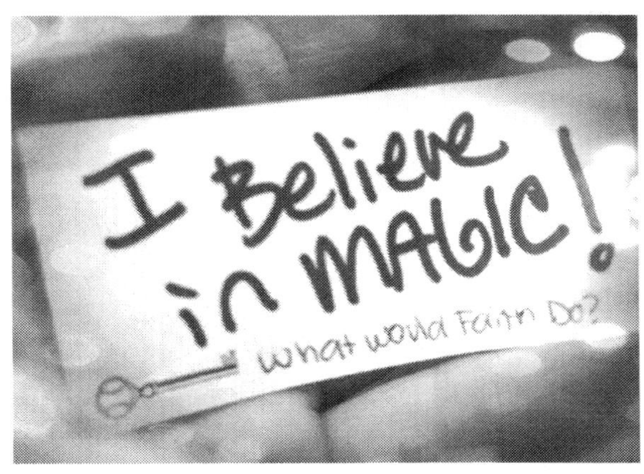


# Introduction: What Would Faith Do?

Growing up, my mom was not much of a storyteller. Even today you will not hear her say, "When you were young…" or "I remember when…" Yet, I've always been curious about my name. My sisters had more mainstream names: Dawn, Wendy, and Heather. There's nothing wrong with those names, but they weren't anything like Faith, Hope, or Charity. I started to wonder if there was something more—maybe a story behind my name. My two older sisters had named our youngest sister, so I assumed they had named me as well. I am thirteen years younger than my second oldest sister, so it made sense that they'd come up with my name.

Out of curiosity three years ago, I emailed my mom to find out why she had named me Faith. I asked her to email me back and tell me the story of how I got my name—this way she could take the time to remember and give me the details. A day or two later she got back to me. Her response was more than I could have imagined, and she *definitely* gave me the full story.

Here's the email she sent:

> Faith,
>
> Well it was kind of a combination of things. At first, Skip and I did not think he could have any children, and it took a long time and faith before you came to be.
>
> Also, when we moved to Pueblo West in 1976, I did not know anyone. I met a lady named Faith who was very helpful and friendly to me.
>
> When you were born, I thought **Faith was a perfect name for you,** because I needed a lot of faith to have you come into my life, and as it turned out over the years, I have needed a lot of faith to keep you in my life.
>
> Love, Mom

I had never heard any of this before. At thirty-three years old, I was getting the complete picture for the very first time. I had known that being named Faith in 1976 was rare, so I'd always felt my name was unique and appreciated it for that reason. The awareness I had about my name, along with my mom's story, made me realize just how perfect and special it was and still is. I also saw that it wasn't until I was ready to receive the story of my name that it came into my life.

I hadn't known that getting pregnant had been difficult for my mom until she told me that story. It felt even more important for me to embrace and honor my name, knowing that it took *faith* for me to come into this world. So, it was not by accident or coincidence that I was named Faith. Even before I was born, *faith* had something to do with powerfully bringing me into this world.

Learning the details of how my name had been chosen has made my life make even more sense. It is this belief in *faith* that makes me know I am supposed to share my story with the world. And I believe I am completely ready now!

It was 2:00 a.m. on a Thursday night. A friend of mine had been pulled over and an hour later found herself in jail for an unpaid speeding ticket. She was definitely not in a good place. Before she knew it, the minutes had ticked by, and she was still sitting in a jail cell at noon on Friday.

She was in one of the most negative places she'd ever found herself. Imagine the negativity, the thoughts, the blame, and everything else that was going through her mind. She realized that if she was going to get through this, she had to switch her attitude. That's when she stopped and asked herself, "What would Faith do? If Faith found herself in this situation, what would she do?" *I know*, she thought, *she'd write 100 things she's grateful for, even those things that haven't happened yet.*

All she had was her admission slip and a pen, so she flipped over the paper and started to write. Her list included things like, "I'm grateful for getting a ride home. I'm grateful for getting released from jail." The list went on and on. She finished her first 100. When she ran out of room on her paper, she started to recite 100 more things she was grateful for *out loud*. Friday, at 4:44 p.m., she got out of jail—just minutes before she would have had to stay through the entire weekend.

She told me this story and said she knew it was the exercise of writing 100 things she was grateful for that shifted her energy and allowed her to get out of jail before the weekend. Being able to be grateful for not only what she already had in her life, but also what she knew was coming, made everything change in her favor. When she shared this story with me, it was a reminder for me to keep spreading love and my message of faith.

I was so inspired by her story that I later shared it with my yoga teacher, who said to me, "That's what your book should be called—*What Would Faith Do?* And so the book title and the "What Would Faith Do?" movement were born. In knowing how my life inspired and gave my friend strength, I realized that I could invite others to join me in making powerful shifts in their lives.

Over the years, my "jailhouse" friend hasn't been the only one to come back and tell me about times when they found themselves in a bad situation and asked that same question: *What would Faith do*? My friend Brian told me that I'm there for him even when I don't know it. But really, it's not about me. It's not about what *Faith Young* would do—it's about, "What would *faith* do?"

What I want for YOU and the seven billion people on this planet is to know that I believe in you. And I want you to believe in YOU too. I want you to have that spark in your life—to rekindle what you already know about yourself and to become who you were meant to be. I want you to live through love, gratitude, and appreciation for the love and abundance in your life.

My job is to be a teacher and messenger and introduce you to what I call, "Tools of Faith." These tools of faith are much like a portal—once you know about them, you can access and put them to use at any time. You don't have to wait years for change to happen. There is no need to wait—you can implement these tools immediately. You can wake up tomorrow morning and have an action plan for how to change your life. In response to my passion, each day more and more people are becoming a part of spreading the love and joining the movement to live their lives through the power of love and abundance. You can too. I invite you to join the movement by sharing your story on the "What Would Faith Do?" blog.

**Now, how does it get any better than that?!**

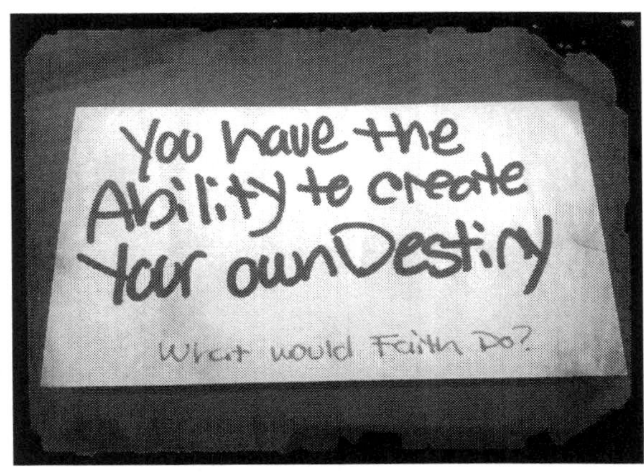


# Chapter 1: You Create Your Own Destiny

"If I end up in the emergency room, who is even going to care, let alone notice?" I spoke those words out loud, not fully knowing or understanding the impact they would have on my life just a few days later.

There I was, a troubled eighteen-year-old kid. My life was consumed with violence, negativity, and pain. It was literally all I knew. I'd been raised in a family that based everything on violent actions and negative emotions. How was I supposed to know anything else? So I acted in alignment with what I had been taught. I was violent. I was negative. And I was in pain.

Growing up in my home had been a struggle. My mom worked three jobs just to make ends meet, and she wasn't home much. At the very young age of eight years old, I was responsible for taking care of my baby sister and myself. That meant getting us up for school, getting us to and from the bus stop, cooking dinner for the two of us, cleaning up, and then getting both of us ready and into bed—all before my mom got home from work. I was forced to grow up fast.

My household was not a loving, caring place either. I can remember waking up in the middle of the night to my parents fighting—yelling and screaming at each other. I lived in constant fear, listening to statements like, "I hate you! I wish you would die!" And these were just some of the words I heard.

At the age of fifteen, I ran away from home, because I finally realized that I couldn't endure the physical, mental, and emotional abuse any longer. I knew that the pain and suffering I saw growing up wasn't right. I knew there had to be another way to care for a family. I left the state, which I can now see was a cry for help. I was searching for something to relieve all that pain. I ended up being "missing" for three weeks. And, instead of getting the help I so desperately needed, that experience only brought more pain and suffering. It taught me that if someone has the courage to reach out, it's important for me to have the strength to reach back!

By the time I was a teenager, all I knew was how to yell and scream and physically and emotionally hurt other people. That is what I had seen growing up and that is exactly what I did. And man, did I know how to do it! Even to a fault. Though I intended to protect myself and others, I violently lashed out at the world. It didn't matter who I hurt while I looked out for me or others.

As an example, I had three restraining orders against me from fellow high school classmates. If I heard a person picking on someone else, I'd step in and kick the shit out of them, just to prove that they shouldn't be doing it. It was my way of trying to protect others, my way of empowering both me and the ones I was protecting. It's not something I'm proud of, but it was who I was, created out of the thoughts I had carried about what was possible for me.

So, let's consider the space I was in when I asked the question, "Who's going to care?" By the time I was a senior in high school, I had already moved out of my mom's house and into my boyfriend's, continuing in a vicious cycle of abuse with him. We had very unhealthy fights, and I found myself yelling and screaming, which only invited even more abuse. Here I was—a high school senior—overwhelmed and working forty hours a week, just to take care of myself. I grasped on to any attention I could get, whether it was good or bad.

Just days after I had asked that question out loud, I was driving down a side street on a cold March night and rolled my Bronco one-and-a-half times. Everything in the Bronco was thrown out of the windows, except for me. My purse, my first flip cell phone, all of it ended up underneath this heaping pile of metal. By the time the sheriff arrived, I had escaped by crawling out of the window. Broken glass had shattered all around me, looking much like my life at that time. I remember the sheriff asking me, "*You* came out of that pile of metal? Is there another person dead inside?"

In that moment, I realized that I had just given myself the biggest gift. I looked around me, turned back towards the accident, and stared at my Bronco. I couldn't believe I was walking away from this scene, heading to the ER, but all in one piece. *Had this really just happened*? Yes it had, and I knew instantly that I had created it. Right then and there, I understood that my thoughts create things. I thought, *If all of the negativity and scarcity I've lived with so far in my life could create an accident like this, imagine what that much positive energy could create!*

My mind was spinning. Right there in that very moment I said to myself, *Oh my God! I created this car accident. I was just asking myself that if I ended up in the ER, who would even care, let alone show up. Well, here I am! Because of all the pain, all the negativity in my life thus far, all I've ever expected were bad things to happen to me*. That was all I'd ever known.

The good news was that there were people who did show up, people who cared. That's when I began to take ownership of my thoughts and said to myself, *If I could create, with my negative thoughts, a horrible car accident that would land me in the ER, what else could I create*? *Imagine if I actually created positive events instead of traumatic ones*. The seed was planted. From that day on, the Faith Young I had been was no longer.

The awareness came instantly, but it did take time to see how this might look in my life. After the accident, I needed to have knee surgery. I also wore a night guard to help the TMJ I suffered as a result of the accident, and I saw a chiropractor three times a week for the whiplash

I'd experienced. Over the following year-and-a-half, I dealt with these issues along with migraines. With the help of biofeedback, I learned how to relieve myself of my migraines. By focusing on the energy in my hands and creating heat in them, I was able to take the extra energy away from my brain and remove my own migraine—a technique I still use today. Through that time of healing, I learned even more deeply that my mind had the power to heal me and to create things.

This accident was one of the most defining moments of my life. I literally woke up. I became aware. Overnight, my rock-bottom life shifted into something more. As I made sense of it all and decided to change how I showed up in life, even more awareness came to me. I realized that the more I was aware of what was *really* going on in my life, the more I was able to see how powerful I was as a human being. As a younger teenager, I'd pushed down thoughts like these. In the past, I'd been misunderstood and even considered a little crazy by some, but after the accident I began to trust my thoughts more and more.

Everything happens for a reason. Every single thing, good or bad, is a part of our journey. It's there to teach us, guide us, and shape us so that we can live our true destiny and purpose. Obstacles appear in our life to act as reminders and mirrors of the truth we were born with, which we may have lost along the way. You see, each of us, every person on this planet, came into this world already knowing their path and purpose.

At fifteen, I was young and very angry. I hated my mother during that time, my baby sister hated me, and everything was a mess. But it was what I had to go through to gain the understanding and awareness to be where I am today. I could blame my mother and father for how they parented us, but I don't. If I did, I'm sure I wouldn't be writing this book. I'd be sitting at Starbucks, wondering why everything happened *to me,* playing the victim, choosing abusive men, having bad friendships, and making bad business decisions. Life doesn't happen *to you.* You choose it so you can learn from it and receive the greatest gifts from the experiences you need in order to be and have more.

A few years after that rollover car accident, I went to a friend's get-together. She planned some cool things for her party and even invited a medium to do readings for people. At twenty-one, I was still going through changes, and I was open to new ideas and excited about new possibilities, learning that there were other ways to live rather than how I'd grown up. When my friend told me the medium would be there, I knew immediately that I wanted to have a reading done. I was intrigued and willing to experience new things.

I sat down with this woman and made the decision to be as open as possible with her. I had no idea or any expectations about what she would tell me. In my time with her, she spoke the most powerful pieces of wisdom I'd ever heard—exactly everything I needed to hear.

"Faith," she said, "you chose to be born to your parents."

*What*? Had I just heard her correctly? *No way. Why*

*would I have chosen my parents*? "Did I just hear you correctly?" I wanted to be sure I had.

"Yes, Faith. We all choose our parents."

*I chose them*?

Surprisingly, my grandfather came to me through the medium. He had been my only grandfather, and when I was very young he'd behaved inappropriately with me. My grandfather passed away when I was twelve. His funeral had been a very negative and traumatic experience for me, because of what I'd been forced to do.

My grandparents were Catholic, so the services took place in the Catholic Church. As part of the church's ritual, everyone was supposed to go up to the casket and touch the body. I have been able to see auras since I was very little (something my family tried to convince me I wasn't really seeing). As they pulled me towards the casket, I could see images of blackness around the casket. I could feel death. I begged for my family to not make me touch him and to let me back away. Yet, they dragged me up there and made me put my hand to his body. As a result of that experience, I didn't go to another funeral for twenty years. When my grandma passed away, I attended her funeral, but I had to have some extra help in order to be comfortable during her service. They closed her casket before I entered the room, and after the service I was escorted out before they reopened it.

The message my grandfather gave me through the medium was, "This is all part of your path to become what you were meant to be." Time seemed to slow down and even stand still as I processed what he was saying through this woman. I knew that his message referred to everything I'd experienced growing up. I knew that it was about my mother and father as well as what had happened to me with him. *This was all part of my path*? *None of this was meant to destroy me*? *All of it actually happened so I could find my true direction*? In that moment, I felt layers of emotion being lifted. Shame. Guilt. Grief. Anger. Blame. Resentment. I knew it was time for me to take complete ownership of my life and stop blaming the circumstances of my life on my family and my surroundings.

More than anything, I felt forgiveness. I could forgive my grandfather for what happened to me when I was very small. I could forgive my father for leaving and my mom for kicking me out and not protecting me. I could forgive both my parents for all of the abuse and hardship I had experienced growing up. I could even forgive the guy who raped me when I was fifteen. At that moment, I knew I could forgive all that had happened to me and not blame anyone for any of it. Most of all, I knew I could forgive myself. I understood that everything that had happened was meant to help me find my path. I still didn't know what my path was, but I did know in that instant that there was both a purpose and a reason for everything that had taken place.

I knew going forward from then on that I could eliminate blame and take ownership for whatever happened in my life, which made the ongoing act of forgiveness possible. I could accept that I chose this path, so much so that I chose it even before I was born. I chose my parents in order to experience the pain I needed to go through so that I could become who I was meant to be. Whatever was yet to come, I chose that too. Just like my mom had said, it took a lot of faith being me in this world.

My perspective shifted so fast that I could hardly comprehend what was happening. All I knew is that when I embraced these truths and this new piece of wisdom, I felt empowered. It meant that I could start to see all of my life in a different way, including all the hurt from my parents and everything that happened as a kid. I could stop being a victim and start taking ownership for it all. I could stop blaming my family for my life. The veil was lifted, and once again a new awareness was brought to my attention.

Some years later, when I attended a three-day event with Greg Mooers, he told the group that we must eliminate blame if we want to change our life. I realized that I'd done it years earlier—that I'd taken ownership and stopped blaming my life on my family long ago. It was even more freeing to know that as a young adult I had let all that blame and resentment go. His statement confirmed for me that I'd stopped being a victim years earlier.

Your life experiences are simply there to guide you, to remind you of who you are. They are there to challenge you and to make you uncomfortable so you can seek out your purpose and your path. You don't need to hit rock bottom to discover who you really are—you can pay attention to all the signs, symbols, chaos, challenges, and heartache you experience along the way and find the answers. All your experiences have happened for a purpose—whether within your family or the community you were raised in, even whether or not you felt empowered or disempowered—and all of it was for your own benefit. They are what I call whispers from the divine—those moments in your life when you are being guided and led down the path to your purpose and calling.

These moments and experiences are reminders and hold the answers you are seeking. The whole meaning of our existence is for us to find our path and discover what is important to our own life. Our families, however dysfunctional, are here to help us reconnect with who we are and who we are meant to be. We were born with a purpose, yet we may have lost sight of it along the way, but when we begin to look at our life experiences, our core purpose will begin to make sense.

Because each of us comes into this life with a chosen purpose, two people can simultaneously experience the same events, yet perceive them in a completely different way. That perception can affect their self-value and how they view their life, including whether or not they feel they are being violated or validated. That perception will help define them. How they each choose to allow the experience to define them will be up to their reaction to it.

Take ownership of everything that happens or has happened to you. When you do this, it gives you power. You may be asking, *I chose to be abused, neglected, etc.?* It was there to help you understand who you are and who you are meant to be. Don't question it. Whose fault it is doesn't matter. Blaming won't get you anywhere. Say to yourself, "I chose this path. I needed this experience. This will help me discover who I am meant to be. It is a gift."

Life does not happen *to you*. There are no accidents, no coincidences. You have the choice in life—to create more, to learn from it, to grow. It's all a gift, all for your purpose. That purpose was with you from the beginning—you were born with it in its rawest form.

**Ask yourself, "What do I want more of?"**

Although somewhere along the path, with all the noes and shoulds and musts, we can get knocked off track from our purpose; we never lose it—not completely. There is more to life for us to create. We all want more. It is our human nature. And it's tied to our life purpose.

Do you want more from your life? You can create it. You have the ability to create your own destiny.

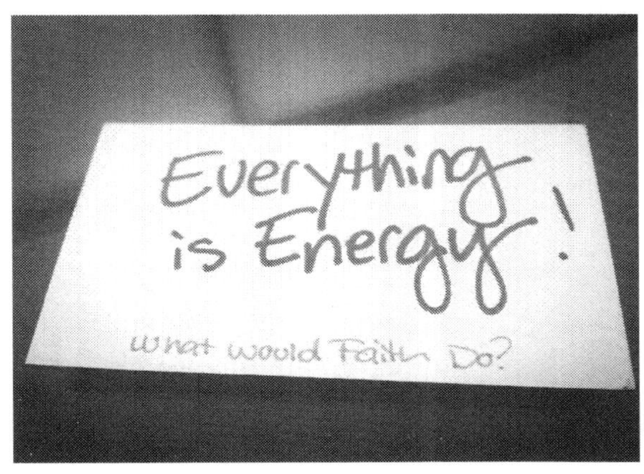


# Chapter 2: It's All About Energy

We are all connected by energy. Our thoughts, feelings, and actions all create energy. We are energy ourselves. Even the trees, the chair we sit on, and the stuff we own are all energy. Energy, although we can't always see it, is there. It's in everything.

A shift has begun to happen in our perception and understanding of energy. Human beings are becoming more aware of energy—that it is in us and in all that surrounds us. As the world continues to shift, more and more people will be able to see how we are all energy, that we are all connected, and that we are all in this together. A big part of the shift taking place is being able to recognize that energy.

Energy has always been here. Thousands of years

ago, people acknowledged energy, even when they couldn't really understand it or make sense of it. Sadly though, today, because of technology and where we've gone with our technological "advances," most people have distanced themselves from energy. Not only can technology distance our connection to energy, it can also keep us distanced from each other. However, when we stay in tune with energy, it is possible for us to have a higher connection with those around us.

To get a physical experience of energy, think about a really hot day you've experienced in the past, the kind of day where the heat was almost unbearable. Do you remember looking at your car after it had been sitting out in the sun, exposed to the heat of the day? Do you recall the vapors as they rose from your car's hood? That is how I like to describe energy. You can't always see it, but there are times when it becomes visible or takes on a physical form. The heat you saw rising off the hood of the car was energy being emitted, and in that instance, you could see it. That energy was always there, even when you couldn't see it, but the excessive heat made it visible.

We're all energy. And if we're aware of that energy, we can use it to help ourselves and others—to do good for everyone. The more we understand energy, the more we can take ownership of our own and be aware of the energy of other people. But, in being aware of the energy around us, we don't have to take on anyone else's energy. Instead, our awareness can help us send others the love they need. We have the ability and the power to love and support each other through the use of our energy.

Everything we do involves energy. Since there is energy in everything, the energy of what we want or don't want is always there too, ready to tap into. Have you ever had the experience of thinking about someone and then they call? It's because they can pick up, or sense, your energy. Or, have you ever thought about someone, only to find out later that they were going through a tough period or something else significant was happening in their life? Don't chock this up to coincidence; nothing in life is coincidence. It's all energy.

Energy is so powerful that I believe people are afraid of it. A lot of times, people deny it because it seems too scary to consider. Yet, it can be so inspirational and create so much positivity and so many miracles that I wonder why we try to steer clear of it.

When I had a mastermind group called Master Manifesting, we got together for collective thoughts, or as some might call it, collective prayer. This happens when you get a group of people together in the same room and each person says what they want. The group then becomes the collective to aid in the manifestation of your vision. In our mastermind group, there were ten of us, so every expressed desire was intensified tenfold.

As a result of this mastermind group, my girlfriend Alex found her soulmate. We helped her with what I like to call "creating space." We created space for it to happen, and she manifested him within weeks. Within months, she had moved in with him, and they then married within the same year. Now, that is the power of collective thought!

As we did in our group, each person in the group

shares their desire with the others, and it then becomes a collective thought amplified by the number of people present—as if the pawns on the chessboard are being rearranged to create what we want. Imagine what can happen when a million people are focused on the same collective thought. That's energy!

One of my favorite ways to work with energy is to send loving thoughts to others. I make an effort by saying it: "I'm sending my love." What I am doing is sending good energy to that person. And what I send out to them is likely to come back to me. And, whenever someone says they are sending me love, I immediately respond with, "I can FEEL it!" Because I am in tune with energy, I CAN feel it.

Our typical response when someone treats us badly or does something to hurt us is to wish bad things on them. Remembering, though, that what we send out comes back, if we send out hate, or negative energy, that kind of energy is what will potentially be returned to us. That's why sending love is more powerful, because it can create more of what you want in your own life instead of more of what you don't want.

## Your Energy Supply

I used to say that I had an unlimited supply of energy, and a friend of mine said, "Faith, that's bullshit! You are a human being. You are here for a limited time." I realized she was right. "No, no," I responded, "the *Universe* has an unlimited supply of energy." So now I say, "I will recharge my batteries." (Note: when I use the word "Universe," insert whatever word feels right for you in reference to the divine.)

**To learn more about this, check out the Global Consciousness Project online.**

Every day when we take a nap, get a good night's sleep, go jogging, or even go to the spa—which is my favorite thing to do—any of these activities re-feed and refuel our energy. Just like the juice needed for your iPhone, these actions give you juice.

My friend Dale taught me that, like a battery, we only have 100% of energy each day, and if we allow our energy to be depleted by someone else, for instance, by engaging in a fight or dealing with something that went wrong, that leaves us with only a portion of our energy left—for us and everyone we interact with throughout the rest of the day. The more intense the situation, the less energy we'll have remaining. So, managing our energy and recharging our batteries are essential to taking care of ourselves *and* others.

Sometimes you might have a sense that someone is trying to tap into your energy supply, but at the end of the day, you have total control over your energy. No one can take yours from you. Only you can allow yours to get depleted. So, it's important to be aware of who you spend time with and what happens when you're together.

If you find yourself saying, for instance, "Every time I go out with Jane Doe, I feel exhausted afterwards," you might need to look at what goes on when you're with her. Do you find that you spend the entire time trying to lift her up, to make her feel better? Or do you need to keep your own guard up because she becomes toxic and overly critical? If you find yourself doing anything that looks like either of these scenarios, you're probably being depleted energetically. In trying to engage with them, your own reserve runs dry and you can feel as if they have sucked the life right out of you. By managing your energy, and being aware of who you spend time with, you will be able to see when your cup is running low and needs to be filled back up. As you manage your own energy more consciously, you can then provide more energy for the people you choose to be with.

## Embrace Your Energy

People give off energy. The more we embrace our energy, the bigger it gets and the more we have to give. Most people, though, operate in an energy field that is about the size of an eight-inch circle around their heart. They hold their energy tightly to themselves, keeping it inside that space at their core rather than allowing it to flow outward. However, when we keep it too close to ourselves; we can't experience anything bigger. We don't allow ourselves to expand, which means we can't give and we can't receive. There is no energy exchange. The more you embrace your energy and allow it to expand, the bigger it gets.

Some people's energy is bigger than others—some people can get really expansive. You can engage and expand your own energy by allowing it to go outside and beyond your body, or outside that average eight inches around your heart. Here's an exercise to practice: Picture a ball of red energy around your heart. Now, make that ball of energy even bigger, as big as your whole chest. Can you feel the energy in your chest? Now, move it through your whole body. It feels like a ray of sunshine, so allow that warmth to come through your skin and move outward, as if you're standing outside on a warm summer afternoon. Now your energy is surrounding your entire body.

You can adjust your energy as you feel it, expanding or contracting it as necessary. The more you allow your energy to be outside your body, the more powerful connections you can make. When you embrace your own energy and allow it to expand, believe me, people will notice. Unfortunately, they'll also notice if your energy is not very big.

Have you ever felt invisible or wondered why you didn't notice someone else in the room? It was likely because they had their energy contained, maybe even hidden or stuck right around their heart. Then again, have you ever immediately felt someone's presence when they walked into a crowded room? That's energy as well—big energy from someone who understands energy and allows it to expand.

When someone walks in with the intention to be expansive, to have connection and share their love, you can sense it. You might not be sure what it is, but you can feel it. That person is holding their energy, yet sharing it. When someone's energy is big and vibrating, we notice. It's how those of us who know how to embrace our energy get heads to turn. Most people don't even know what it is that's making them turn their heads towards us—but it's energy.

## Checking Yourself at the Door

When I have a bad day, it's like an enormous neon light blazing for all to see. People can feel it from a mile away. I've learned that's what happens for me, and I manage it. When I feel this way, I like to do something I call "checking myself at the door." If I'm having a bad day, I try to balance myself and release any of that negative energy before I enter a room or before I meet with someone, because I know that that energy will affect the other person, whether I intend for that to happen or not.

To balance myself, I put both feet on the ground and consciously ground with the Universe. I try to neutralize my energy by saying, "Let me give any negative energy back and attract more positive, calming energy from the Universe." It doesn't always work, because sometimes I'm still unconsciously holding on, but more times than not, I truly am able to check myself at the door.

## Your Energy Can Affect Others

When I'm having a positive day, which I try to have most of the time, people love it because they too walk out having a great day. When someone has coffee with me, they don't even know why, but they often leave feeling on top of the world. It's because that's how I came in. Everyone's energy is contagious. The energy that you bring and give off affects other people, whether you want to admit it or not.

Even if someone is not directly in your proximity, your

energy can directly affect another. For instance, I was out for Halloween this past year and someone keyed my car. Instantly, I thought, *That's not right*. I immediately commanded myself to take ownership of the situation. *What had I been doing recently? Had I been putting out positive energy? Or was there something I'd done that could have brought this on?* I knew I couldn't change this situation, but I could take a moment to reflect on the immediate past to see if there was a connection to my recent behavior, thoughts, or actions. Since I knew everything happens for a reason, I had to take a moment to consider how I'd behaved recently—if I'd been putting out that kind of negative energy, then that's what I would have attracted back to me.

I also thought that whatever energy I give out in the world as a result of this incident will come back tenfold. So instead of being angry, I said, "Let me send them some love, because they are going to need it." I knew something was also going to come back to them tenfold. Whenever anyone puts out that much negativity, that negative energy will come back to them. Because I understood the impact our energy can have on one another, I also considered what I wanted to put into the world at that moment. It is hard when someone does something hurtful to us, but we have to be mindful of what we do in response and what we want to create "more of" in our own lives.

Although I understood that this person had crossed a line, and initially I felt anger towards them, I was sure I didn't want to respond from that anger. In situations such as this, I ask questions like: "What do you think their intention was? Is this about me or about them?" When I get to a point that I am angry, I know it's because I've allowed the circumstances to make me angry. At those times, I ask, "What can I do to change this situation?" We can allow ourselves to be angry or hurt, but rather than get stuck there or react from that place, we can ask ourselves why we're angry and then go deeper to see what we can do with those feelings to shift them.

There are times when it's difficult to understand what another's intentions are. I don't believe anybody I encounter during my day wakes up the morning and says, "How can I screw over Faith today?" But, boy, do people sometimes act like that's exactly what they're trying to do. So, it's important that each of us choose our actions carefully. And when I do encounter an unpleasant situation, I often ask the person directly what their intentions were. The results are usually really beautiful, because most people have good intentions and often don't realize how they're coming across.

We all control our own energy, but our energy can also be influenced by the energy of others or our surroundings. While I didn't necessarily create my car getting keyed, there might have been some other energy that influenced what happened, whether that had been around me or around where my car had been that night. Sometimes we can't explain the events that happen—sometimes they're part of a bigger picture. We don't always know the reasons why things happen, but if we can understand that they're part of something much bigger than we are, we can remind ourselves that we don't need to know the why. Instead, we can ask ourselves what we can learn from what's taken place.

## Who You Spend Time With

It goes to show that it's really important to manage who you spend time with, because both positive and negative people will influence your life. If someone is negative, you might have to release them from your life. For instance, I had a friend who was an important part of my life during my divorce. Years later, I realized how negative she was. She had been a great friend through my divorce, and the sounding board I needed during that time, but eventually I had to let her go. I was ready to move on and improve my life, but she wanted me to continue to play victim along with her.

As soon as I made a shift away from my marriage and towards a new life for myself, we no longer served each other, and I found I couldn't spend any more time with her. I truly believe that when we realize a relationship is not serving us, or when that relationship is even trying to take us backwards, it takes more courage for us to walk away from it than to stay. In my situation, I knew her negativity would bring me down ten times faster than my positive energy could bring her up. And so we parted ways.

Being aware of how you are affected by energy and how you are affecting others with yours is essential to creating more in your life and fulfilling your purpose. If you know your energy is to empower people, then make sure you are in that space and energy when you are around people.

## Protecting Your Energy

There will be times when you get around people or situations that have the potential to drain your energy, so knowing how to protect your energy is essential too. You can protect and preserve your energy by putting up an imaginary barrier around you and your body. When you do this, it becomes difficult for someone to penetrate your energy.

In my world, I call it a ball of fire. When I have that barrier up, I know it will take a lot for people to get through it. At the same time, I want to be translucent, being vulnerable and allowing people to see me for who I am in order to allow good energy in.

You need to be aware that if you put up a wall to block energy, you could also be blocking positive energy, so be clear about why you're creating a barrier. For instance, if you find that you've been allowing someone to drain your energy, you can put that wall up to block their energy. First, ground yourself with the earth, which is full of energy. The earth is a neutralizer, so anytime you send anything back to the earth, it neutralizes; it doesn't go back as negative energy. To completely ground yourself, just imagine a cord from your tailbone extending far into the earth, or simply feel your feet beneath you and imagine being locked in or held down by the earth.

**Protect your energy by creating a barrier around yourself and then ground yourself to the earth.**

Next, you can use a Hawaiian

prayer I love, which is, "I am sorry. Please forgive me. I love you. Thank you." It's a ho'oponopono mantra and is said to heal and cleanse all levels and in all directions of time and space. It's a healing prayer for energy and perfect to use when you need to protect yours.

In this ho'oponopono prayer, it states, "Please forgive me." If this statement doesn't sit well with you, you can choose not to include it, because I believe if your intention is to truly do everything out of love, then you should never have to ask for forgiveness. But if your intentions weren't pure, allow your ego to "come down" and say this statement for the highest good of all. Now remember, when reciting this prayer, you don't actually say it directly to the person—you say it energetically. You might even want to write it in a journal.

My twist on this prayer is that at the end of it I add, "I ask for all my energy back from you, and in return, I send all your energy back to you." So, send that other person love, ask for all your energy back, and give all their energy back to them. That's one of the most powerful things you can do for yourself and your energy. Although people can't take your energy away unless you allow it, this is a way to consciously let the Universe know you want to make sure each of you has your own energy—you ask to release and be released.

It's the same when someone leaves your life—always ask for your energy back and give that person back their energy. It's the way to refill your cup. When someone leaves our life or disappoints us, we often say to ourselves, "I just spent a lot of time and energy on them and now they are walking away." What we're really saying is that we feel we just gave a lot of ourselves away to that other person. To change that energy and emotion, we can ask for our energy back. It's how we can continue to provide support to others and manage our own energy without being drained. If our cup is half full, how can we expect to fill up someone else's cup? We have to fill our own cup first!

**Is Your Energy Outside of Your Body?**

Have you stumbled, tripped, fallen,
or bumped into a wall? That's the Universe's
way of telling you that you are off track.
If you don't listen, you might spill
your coffee or get into a fender-bender.
Pay attention to your initial clumsiness and
check your energy (at the door!).
Ask: Where are my thoughts right now?

## Time and Energy

Have you ever thought about how humans created time and the clock? We needed to make sense of why the sun came up and went down, and so we created a clock and what we now call time. Yet, time is a perspective. For example, I only require five hours of sleep, because for me that's more than enough.

What if you operated from a place of belief that there was more than enough time for everything that happens? When I hear people say, "I am too busy," or "I'm so busy that I don't have any time," what I really hear is that they don't want more. They have enough. They are full. Those words are powerful, and the Universe hears you and responds. How can you receive more if you are already full, if you already have enough?

**What you think about, you bring about.**

Time is all in your perspective, and your words are powerful. Think about traffic for a minute. Picture yourself driving to a meeting and you realize you will be a few minutes late. Notice the words you say to yourself. Likely it sounds like, "I'm late, I'm so late, I'm running behind, I'm going to be late." Next time you find yourself "running late," try changing your language or shifting your perspective. Say instead, "There's plenty of time. I'm always on time." You'll find the traffic eases up, lights turn green, and you arrive with more ease. Poof! It's that easy.

## Redirecting Energy

Other people's energy influences us all the time, so you need to know whether it's your energy affecting you or someone else's. Being aware and present are essential. If you are tired, ask yourself, "Is that really me? Am I really tired or is the person in the car with me the one who is tired?" Their energy is strong enough to influence you.

By being aware, you can create changes that benefit you. For instance, if someone else is tired, and it's not you, send that person back their tired energy. Tell yourself then that you are full of energy. Check yourself throughout the day to see where your energy levels are; are they positive or negative, full or running low? Are they what you want to feel or what you don't want to feel?

## Shifting Energy

Once, I got into a fight with a boyfriend and decided I needed to escape, so I went into the bathroom to take a bath. Instead of staying and fighting, like I would have done ten years earlier, I wanted to go and take some time for myself. I wanted to reflect on why we were fighting and why I was allowing him to take my energy away.

While I was in the bath, he came in and said, "I'm outta here." Realizing he was in such a negative place and feeling so exhausted from dealing with his negative energy, I replied, "Cool. Have fun. I'll see you later."

After I got out of the bath, I went to do my nightly ritual of putting money in jars, and I couldn't believe what I found. Apparently, when he left the bathroom, he decided to steal from me by taking the money I had been saving in my money jars. I had worked hard to put money in those jars every day. Some days it was just a few dollars, but I had saved $175, which was a lot of money to me at the time.

I was completely devastated when I realized he had taken everything out of them. He knew what that money meant to me, yet he took it anyway. Based on my past and all the people who had betrayed my trust, all those who had hurt me—most especially men—his actions broke my heart. What he did brought up a lot of old feelings for me. Why would someone so close to me hurt me so badly? I fell to my knees in total despair. Then, I thought to myself, I have to do something to shift my energy. What will happen tomorrow if I don't check this energy at the door? So, I did what I always do and started to write what I was grateful for. It was one of the hardest lists I've ever written. I got about twenty-seven things, everything from, "I'm grateful he didn't take my life" to "I'm grateful he didn't take my car" to "I'm grateful he didn't take my credit cards." By morning, I was in total gratitude for the experience that had just happened. I was able to shift my energy from scarcity to abundance, and I came to realize that he needed the money more than I did. I was also grateful that an energy shift so large allowed me to release him from my life and move forward in a positive direction.

Your brain can't feel two feelings at once. The number one way to get yourself out of a negative funk is to create a positive atmosphere, and gratitude is such an easy way to do it. You can't feel gratitude and anger at the same time. You can't feel appreciation and scarcity at the same time. You can only feel one or the other. So shifting your feelings is a great way to immediately change the energy.

## Everything is Energy

Knowing you have your own energy and understanding how powerful it can be is essential to your day-to-day success. Be aware of this gift of energy. Know that you can create it, give it, send it, and receive it.

People don't usually realize how influential their energy is to their daily life. Start to notice when things have a ripple effect and compound more of it. Instead of seeing a bad thing in your life and continuing with that energy and thought, stop and look for what you can be grateful for. When someone inflicts pain on you or someone else, send that person love. The Universe will take care of that person. The worst thing you can do is wish death upon someone. Wish the best for everyone.

When the Aurora shooting tragedy occurred at the movie theater here in Colorado, I was on vacation near the ocean. I was hundreds of miles away from Colorado when this terrible event happened, yet even from where I was I could feel it. I felt people's pain—I experienced a heavy feeling of sadness inside and a deep sense of loss. Since I don't watch television or the news I didn't know why I was feeling what I was, but awhile later, I found out through Facebook that a friend of mine had passed away in that tragedy.

I saw that my friend Brian was reaching out for support on Facebook, and I called him immediately. It was about 6:00 a.m. in Colorado when I reached him. He told me he was feeling extremely sad, but he also knew that if it hadn't been for me, he wouldn't have even known Rebecca, the mutual friend who'd been killed. He also told me that because he'd learned from me to tell people who are important in his life that he loves them, his last words to her seven days before the tragedy had been "I love you." This brought tears to my eyes. At least my friend's last words were "I love you." And to know I had an impact on that happening moved me.

Once I got off the phone, I felt even more strongly the pain I had been picking up on—his pain as well as my own. For someone so young and so full of love to be taken out of this world by such hatred saddened me. A few hours later, I found myself at the ocean with that overwhelming feeling and energy of loss. Within moments, I literally lost my sunglasses. I felt such an overwhelming sense of physical loss from losing my expensive prescription sunglasses that I had an explosive temper tantrum right there on the beach. When I told my friend Brian a week later, he said I was just attached to the material item and I replied back, "No, I was thinking about all the loss in Aurora and I lost my sunglasses." I realized that it wasn't about my sunglasses at all. I needed a reason to allow myself to feel the grief and sadness of the energy around me. At first Brian couldn't relate to the feelings of loss that I was experiencing and its connection to physical loss, but that same night he lost his cell phone. Our experiences of loss and the energy attached to them were so strong that we recreated that loss over and over again in our own lives.

If you wake up on the wrong side of the bed, immediately check your energy before you walk out that door. Otherwise, everything could go wrong for the rest of the day. As we learned in physics, energy cannot be eliminated—it can only be transformed. If you don't change that energy immediately, it will continue to attract the same energy to you. Change your energy and you'll change your life.

## Energy Checklist

1. We are all a product of the same energy—we are one energy operating as seven billion people.
2. Some people hold their energy inside of themselves while others project their energy on to others.
3. There is an unlimited supply of energy in the Universe, and we can tap into the Universe's abundant energy any time we want. We can even send unwanted energy back to the Universe!
4. Some people are drawn to energy and some are repelled by it—depending on the energy itself.
5. Energy is neutral, but we make it positive or negative, depending on what we do with it.
6. Everything is energy.
7. We can change our relationships, communities, and society by shifting energy.
8. We can manifest something to happen (positive or negative) by focusing our energy and thoughts.
9. Our negative thoughts can make energy ten times more powerful.
10. Love is the counter to negativity. Send love.

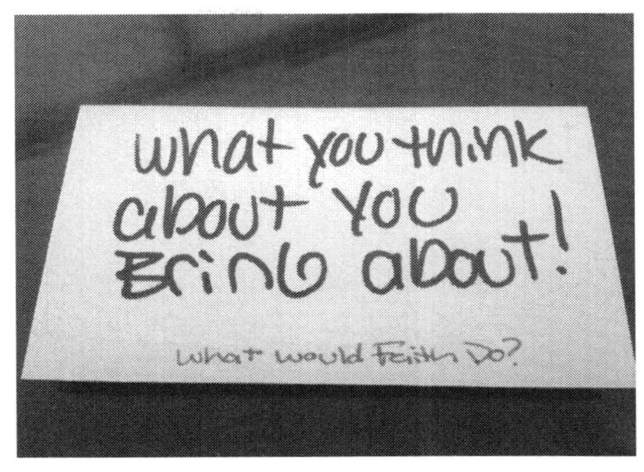


# Chapter 3: What You Think About, You Bring About

Thoughts create things, so what you think about, you bring about. I talked about an example in the last chapter about time and one's perception of being late, but it happens on a bigger scale as well. Your thoughts attract things to you. If you are running late and it throws you off track, then everything throughout your day can snowball—starting from a fight with someone and quite possibly ending with a flat tire. Most people don't connect this sequence of events, but they are all connected by your thoughts.

Two years ago, I was running late for a family function. I was frustrated about being late, and when I arrived at my destination, I got out of my car and my brand new $2,200 MacBook fell out of my laptop bag and right onto the concrete. I was devastated. Thoughts raced through my head. *Oh my gosh, I just got this four months ago. I'm sure it's broken. What will I do? How will I get it fixed?* Dropping my MacBook totally threw me for a loop, so much so that I almost didn't go into the event. Because I am aware of energy and how it can affect what comes next, I didn't want to bring what I was feeling into this next event. I was trying to "check myself at the door" but really struggling. Since I wasn't able to completely let go of what had happened, I stayed through dinner and then left. I went straight home and immediately wrote 100 things I was grateful for.

**Silent gratitude doesn't do anyone any good. Showing your gratitude is essential.**

One of the things I do after writing my "100 things I'm grateful for" is to tell those who appeared on the list. My friend Brian was on the list that night, so I texted him and said, "Hey Brian, I just wrote my 100 things I'm grateful for and you were on the top of my list."

It was about 11 o'clock on a Friday night and he immediately called me and asked, "Faith, is everything all right?"

"Not really," I said.

"What's going on? Do I need to go beat someone up?"

I laughed and told him how my MacBook had fallen out of my car. He replied with, "That's it?"

"Yeah, I've been pretty upset about it, so I started writing down things I am grateful for."

"Well, can I share with you what I was doing?" Brian asked.

Since I know everything is divinely inspired, I told him to please share. His mom was very sick with MS and bedridden. She couldn't move any part of her body below her neck and had been that way for many years. He proceeded to tell me how he had just gotten home and found that his mom had thrown up on herself. He had to get her out of bed, shower her, and then put her back into bed. He'd been sitting in his bed, listening as she cried and exclaimed, "I wish I would just die." He said his eyes filled with tears when he received my text telling him how grateful I was for him.

I was able to be there for him in that really challenging moment in his life. And it was all divinely inspired because my MacBook had fallen out of my car. It goes to show that we shouldn't question when something seemingly "bad" happens—we never know where it will actually take us.

My MacBook was under warranty, so within a few hours the following day I was able to get it fixed. Now, looking back, I can recall that before I dropped my MacBook I'd been thinking thoughts like, *What if something happens to my new MacBook*? I'll be devastated. But it obviously led me to where I needed to be that evening.

## Think About the Message You're Sending

Your reactions to events can clearly tell the Universe what you want or need without you even realizing that you're sending a message at all. For example, if you drop your briefcase on the way out of the office and someone stops to help you and you respond, "No I've got it," you've just rejected their help. Not only have you rejected their offer to assist you, which may be their one gift to put out into the world that day, but you have also just sent a message to the Universe that you don't need any kind of help. So, two hours later, when you get a flat tire and no one comes to your aid, can you guess why that would happen? It's because of the message you sent earlier—*that you didn't need help!* Most of us don't tie these events together, but they are connected. So, as you go through your day, think about the messages you're sending to the Universe in the actions and reactions you have.

## Change Your Thoughts, Change Your Life

The best thing is to be able to switch any negative thoughts immediately, before they create things. The good thing is that there's a time delay with "what you think about you bring about." If you were to say you wanted a pink elephant and it fell from the sky and landed on your lap, you wouldn't know what to do. You wouldn't have a home for it and you wouldn't have food for it either. So, when you think a negative thought, you have time to change or reverse that thought before it manifests.

When I was eighteen and started to change my life around after my car accident, I questioned how I could train myself to think more positively. I had noticed that I naturally went back to negative thoughts and then spiraled off of them. I realized that I needed a way to redirect myself. In order to do that, I needed an image that

I could think about to help me shift my thoughts more quickly. It would be a way to train myself to not be in my negative mind anymore. I called these my "trigger thoughts" because they became a way to start a positive spiral rather than a negative one. When I started to think a negative thought, I switched that thought to my trigger thought. For quite some time, my trigger thought was, "I'm going to win the lottery." I picked that image because it was easy.

When you think about winning the lottery you don't think of one darn negative thought at the same time. You are thinking of all the good stuff—how you'll pay off your mortgage, or buy your mom a house, or buy yourself a Lamborghini. Your brain immediately goes into all kinds of positive thoughts. For many years, that was the trigger thought I used. Divinely, over the years, I've won a couple thousand dollars in the lottery. (Maybe I should have been more specific and said I wanted to win the big jackpot!) Those little tiny thoughts come true.

**Create a trigger thought to help redirect negative thoughts more quickly. What's something that makes you feel good?**

Setting your intentions every day is key to your success. Each day, my assistant and I sit down together and write out our intentions for the day. There have been times that I've said, "My intention is to get my short sale approved." Within hours, I get an email saying the short sale is approved. Was it going to happen? Probably. Would it have happened on that day? Maybe not. But when you clearly define your intentions, it helps create the life you want.

Instead of just waking up and stumbling through your day, set intentions. What I say is, "I have a lunch appointment, so my intention is to show up exactly how that person needs me to show up." Then, when that lunch appointment happens and they leave feeling like they are on top of the world, I think *Awesome! I was able to set that intention and fulfill it.* That's one thing I do to create positive things in my life every day.

**Write your intentions down daily and check in with an accountability partner to share your intentions. When you write your intentions, you're affirming them.**

Sometimes people wait until the end of the day and then think about what they could've done differently. I believe you need to start straight from the gate. First thing when you get out of bed, say what you are grateful for and set your intentions for the day. Rather than stumble through your day, be intentional! Each and every morning, set your intention, even if it is as simple as, "I want to be open and able and willing to receive today."

The following day, my assistant and I always look at what we manifested and celebrate our accomplishments. By looking at what you've manifested, you solidify what you believe. If you set your intentions every day and then one, or two, or three of those intentions come true, it's important to write them down as a success the next day. It's almost like a game you are playing with the Universe. *What else can I put on here*? *What else can I create*? Instead of seeing these as happening by coincidence or accident, see that you are bringing them about in your own life. Then, reward yourself for what you manifested.

When you have 51% positive thoughts, that 1% is enough to shift your thoughts to the positive side and change your life. It's that slight edge that makes all the difference. And it's that simple. People think I have 98% positive thoughts. Maybe someday I will, but to be able to get to that level takes a lot of discipline. Really, though, all you need is 51% positive thoughts to change your life. How I changed my life when I was eighteen was by changing those thoughts immediately, not waiting for an hour to go by and allowing them to spiral, but by changing them right away. That action continues to create a positive ripple effect in my life.

## Focus on What You Do Want

People have a tendency to focus on the things they don't want. I hear people say, "I don't want to be in debt." "I don't have enough money to pay my bills." Well, if those are the things you focus on, then the Universe will deliver more bills and more debt. Focusing on what you do want, instead of what you don't want, is the most essential ingredient to creating more of what you want in your life. In those same situations you can say, "I'm always taken care of," instead of "I don't want any more debt." Or you can say, "I always have more than enough money," instead of "I need to pay my bills." When the Universe hears the words bills or debt, it doesn't hear that you don't want those things. It only hears those words and then gives you more of what you actually don't want. That's why it's so important to focus on what you do want instead of what you don't.

When I was eight years old, I wrote a long list of all the things I didn't want to do as a parent when I grew up, and I had a very short list of all the things I wanted to do. The "didn't want" list included at least fifteen items, things like "I don't want to wake up my children in the middle of the night to clean my house." But the "do want" list contained only two items—one being, "I want to be a loving and caring mother." When reflecting back to that letter that I created at such a young age, it feels as if focusing on what I didn't want was human nature.

For some reason, we are programmed to focus on what we don't want instead of what we do want. Maybe it's our ego trying to protect us or even some kind of survival mechanism, but what I do know is that my imagination was so limited at that time that I had no idea about all of the positive things I could want and have in my life. The cool thing is, when we realize we're focusing on what we don't want, we can immediately shift our approach to a focus on what we do want. So, as you shift things in your life, an important part of changing the paradigms you've operated from is to change those simple words into what you *do* want.

An old boyfriend used to say to me, "You are so mean to me." And I'd reply with, "Your wish is my command." He didn't like that at all. The thing was, how could I ever be anything more if he believed that was all I ever was to him? I'd explain to him that he needed to tell me what he did want from me. I encouraged him to say things like, "I love it when you..." or "It's great when you are on time." I asked him to tell me what he wanted, not what he didn't want. After a while, he did start asking for what he wanted. Although our human nature takes us to what we don't want, it can be quite simple to change the negative into a positive form.

If you are experiencing struggles in a relationship and you want to make it better, write down all the things you love about that person instead of all the things that upset you. If you wrote down all the things that bothered you about someone, that list would continue to grow bigger and bigger and bigger. Likewise, if you write down everything you love about somebody, it will shift the energy. Once you start that list, you'll keep seeing more things to write down. In this situation, I wrote things I loved about my boyfriend. By doing that, I saw a shift in him. I was then able to see more things I loved about him.

## Focus on What You Can Control

You have to focus on what you can control. You can't control if it's snowing outside, but you can control whether you wake up in enough time to leave the house a little earlier so you can drive more slowly to get somewhere on time.

For example, in real estate, I can't control if an inspection goes well. If there's a foundation crack, I can't magically make it go away. What I can control is how I react to it, how we negotiate the deal, or how many phone calls I make to have other deals under contract, so if that one does fall through I have more seeds planted rather than getting all caught up in what didn't happen. For instance, I make twenty-five calls every single day. I can control how many people I talk to, how many lunches I have, how many houses I show, how many networking groups I attend. I can make other appointments, get other offers, and so on. We can't control outside factors, such as the weather or how someone else treats us, but we can definitely control how we react.

"Life is ten percent what happens to you and ninety percent how you respond to it."
- Lou Holtz

## Focus on What's Going Right in Your Life

A friend told me once, "Faith, you are exactly where you are supposed to be in your life right now." At the time, this was difficult for me to understand, because I was so focused and driven that I was not being present in that moment. I think many of us can relate to the frustration of working so hard and feeling disappointed that we aren't millionaires or more successful, but we have to understand that we are perfectly where we are supposed to be at that time.

Focus on what's going on in your own world. Don't focus on what everyone else is doing.

When you say to yourself, "I'm exactly where I am supposed to be right now," your brain starts to think of the things you have done and what's going right. Instead of beating yourself up by saying things such as, "I should do this or have that, I should be here by now, or I should have one hundred listings, but I only have eight right now," it's important to focus on all that is exactly as it should be—where you are at that very moment. That's the way to realize that you have more than you are even aware of in the present.

## The Right Language

Words are powerful enough to limit or expand you. My friend Andrea said to me, "I feel like there are so many opportunities that are missed every day." That word "missed," so simply stated, was what she was manifesting without even realizing it. All she needed to do was make one slight modification. She had to eliminate one word and change her statement to, "I have so many opportunities every day."

Without even realizing it, we can be creating what we don't want. By thinking about the words we choose and using the right language, we can begin to create a world we love—one that is expansive.

## Ask Yourself Powerful Questions

I believe we have a little person inside of us who is there to protect us. So, I ask that person inside of me—who I like to call "my Little"—questions like, "What do you want to wear today?" It might sound crazy, but it works. I've put on my red shoes because of what I heard back as an answer, and those red shoes picked me up a client that very day. Life is all divinely inspired, so you can ask questions like, "Who should I call right now?" "Who do I need to talk to today?" or "What do I want to eat right now?"

One time I asked myself, "Who should I call right now?" I heard that I should call my friend Maricela. It's amazing how the answers just pop up when you are listening. They always show up. When I called her she said, "I'm so glad you called. I've been meaning to tell you, I just got diagnosed with colon cancer." My heart dropped, and instinctively I asked, "What can I do to help?" She said, "Well you know those positive messages you send out? Could you send me one of those every single day?" *Consider it done*. From then on, every day at 2:00 p.m., I got a reminder on my phone that said, "Send Love to Maricela." Those messages included simple statements like, "I'm sending you love and light" and "I'm picturing you happy and well."

**Don't underestimate the power of the little things you do each and every single day and how they can powerfully impact someone's life.**

Six months later, she came to my office and brought me flowers. She said, "Faith, because of the power of love and you believing in me and sending me inspiration every day, without radiation or chemo you helped me cure myself of cancer." The most powerful thing about her story is that if I ever doubt anything in my life, I go back to that moment in time and say, "If I can help my friend Maricela cure herself of cancer through the power of love, I can do anything."

**Doctor Diagnosis:**
**People believe what their doctors tell them. Just like my dog who was diagnosed with bone cancer. The vet told me he had six months. Sure enough, I believed it and six months later I put him down. You don't have to believe what other people tell you. Your thoughts are yours to choose.**

My friend Maricela believed what was possible. She heard what the doctors told her, but she believed in something else. We saw Maricela as already cured, and we didn't fall into the trap of buying into someone else's belief or negative thoughts. By asking powerful questions, I was able to show up as the gift that Maricela was seeking.

## Take Ownership of Your Thoughts, Environment & Friends

When I was eighteen, I started to feel as though my only direction in life was to be mean or negative because that was the environment I had always been in. I had been a reflection of the people who I had spent my time with. I knew I had to take ownership of the people I hung around with and the thoughts I allowed myself to think. And that is what I began to practice.

When I wanted to attract a good man, a friend recommended I hang around other guys I knew who were great examples of what a good man looked like. I'd hang around my friend's husbands, family members, and anyone else who was a good example of what I wanted to attract in my life. I knew that what you think about you bring about, so I decided, "Why not think about and bring about what I truly want?" As a result, I began to attract more good people into my life by tenfold.

**"You are the average of the five people you spend the most time with." - Jim Rohn**

A friend decided to test me one time and said to me, "Tell me something negative. I see all your positive posts, but you've got to have something negative to say." Off the tip of my tongue rolled out, "What you think about, you bring about."

Take ownership of your thoughts. Most people want to take ownership when they win a door prize and announce, "Look at what I just did!" But when their car breaks down, they want to blame everyone else in the world. It doesn't work like that. You create it all, and when you take ownership of your thoughts, your life will change.

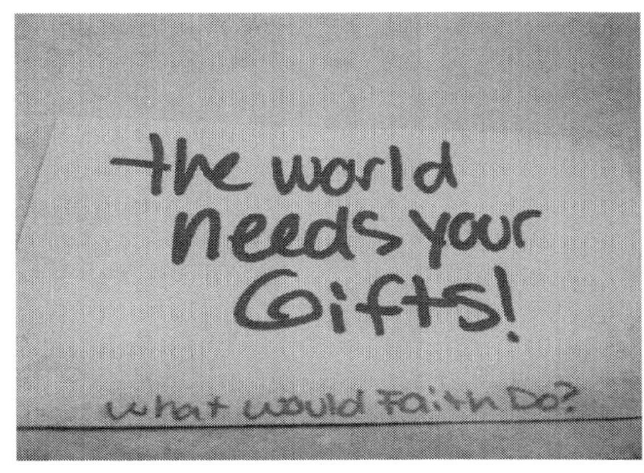

the world
needs your
Gifts!
what would Faith Do?


# Chapter 4: Understanding Your Soul Purpose in Life

We were born with sacred virtues. These sacred virtues help us understand the core of who we are as a human being. Most of us have two or three sacred virtues. They are tied to our core beliefs—those beliefs that are most important to us. Our sacred virtues drive and motivate us. They are what help us fulfill our life's purpose.

When we discover these virtues and really live them, our life opens up to more than we've ever before expected. When these virtues are dishonored or tested, we can get angry, mad, and/or defensive. These virtues are so sacred that they can cause us to break away from our family, our friends, and other people we love.

One way to identify your sacred virtue is to look at what makes you angry about a situation. Other emotions besides anger can also be indicators. Physically, you might feel goose bumps about what you or someone else says or about something that happens. Those goose bumps represent a validation of your virtue. If you find that you are drawn to a particular character in a movie or a book, one you'd love to be and can easily relate to, this may be an indication of one or more of your sacred virtues. It could also be someone you know personally or someone you know about, someone you'd love to be more like—it could be their qualities, strengths, or even their way of living that you're drawn to.

**How to Identify Your Sacred Virtues**

**Look at all the moments in your life where you became extremely enraged and angry. What was being dishonored?**

**Rediscover your sacred virtue by understanding those moments in your life.**

Once you find your sacred virtue, you'll know it. That knowledge makes you feel good. You know it is true from the bottom of your heart. When you discover your virtue, you know very clearly exactly what makes you tick, what pisses you off, what you love, what you like or dislike.

When I was a small child, I saw the same behaviors happen at home—over and over again. My mom would take out all her anger and aggression on my father, and she'd beat him right before our eyes. I hated when she did this. It killed me inside. I wanted my dad to stand up for himself, but I also wanted my mom to help and empower him, not strip his pride away from him.

## A Sneak Peek Into Your Life Purpose

What is your favorite movie character? Or ask yourself, "What character would I be if I could be any character in a movie?"

I'd be Optimus Prime* from Transformers. He is a big strong person who wants to save all the humans. At the end of the movie he sacrificed himself and pulled out his own heart to show that we are all in this together. It's not us against humans; we are all connected.

That's who I am, I want to be the Optimus Prime and save the entire world, and that's my soul purpose.

"Optimus Prime is a heroic, brave, and compassionate character who puts all his talent to use to improve the universe around him. Optimus has a strong sense of justice and righteousness and has dedicated himself to the protection of all life, particularly the inhabitants of Earth; he will battle his foes with unyielding resolve."[1]

---

1. http://galaxyofquotes.sumobaby.net/authors_quotes.php?authorId=119 - Optimus Prime quote

On their anniversary one year, my father stopped at a store to pick up two dozen roses to surprise my mother. He always did what he could to show her love. Instead of being happy about the gesture and his thoughtfulness, she took those roses and beat him with them. Thorns thrashing, petals flying, stems breaking, she berated him for buying something they couldn't afford. I saw the good he was trying to do. That sense of disempowerment ate away at me. It tore me up to see the effects of their relationship on one another and me and my baby sister.

At fifteen years old, I couldn't handle it anymore. I finally took a stand. I stood up to my mother for my father. Her reaction: she kicked me out of the house. I was sent to live with my older sister and her alcoholic husband for nine months. The day after she kicked me out, she kicked my father out too. I have never seen or heard from my father again. That was over twenty years ago. As sad as that was for all of us, it was what my mother needed to get her life back together, to let go of the violence, and for her to become the woman she is today.

When I stood up for my father in such a big way, my mom kicked me out because I wasn't allowed to have a say in the matter. And when my mom threw my father out, she didn't have anyone to take her anger out on anymore. It forced her to change her life, because she had no one else to direct her aggression towards. It was the most powerful decision she could have made for herself.

For the next twenty years, she was not in a relationship, which gave her the chance to work on herself, to really understand where the violence and abuse had come from. She learned that she had been the victim who had unknowingly become the victimizer, and she didn't want either of those roles ever again. She had had enough of being like that.

For a long time, I was angry at my mom for kicking out my father, but now I know that it was for the highest good of everyone. I am even ready to reconnect with my father, but apparently he is not yet ready to do so. I will receive him whenever he is, whether that is in this lifetime or another. I know that I truly love my dad unconditionally.

Have you ever had a moment when you witnessed something where you felt as if you had to step in? It's because your virtue was being violated. And if you didn't say something, you probably said later to yourself, "I should have said something!" I encourage you to say it. You'll feel better because you'll feed your soul and validate what is important to you.

In the woman's group I lead, I had a firsthand account of what happens to someone when their virtues are pushed and tested. In being a part of our group, one of the women began to struggle. There was another woman in the group who was in a similar profession, and the woman who was struggling believed that it was unfair to have this other woman in the group. She saw the woman as a threat to her own security. As the struggling woman's virtues of integrity and justice were being pushed, she became overly negative and dramatic. As a result, it became apparent that she wasn't getting anything out of the group, and she certainly wasn't able to give anything back to the group either. I had tried to give her a warning and asked that she be a positive contributor to the group in order to bring value to all of us. The last straw, after nothing changed, was to let her go. It took a lot of courage to ask her to leave the group, but it was what needed to happen—it was what was best for everyone, including her.

I took a stand for myself and the others, and I asked her to leave. Her negativity was draining for the entire group and definitely not helping any of us. There was an unexpected gift as a result of this change. A few months ago, I ran into a friend of mine who shared with me what this woman had told her recently. The woman had thought she needed me to change her life, and she tried to hold on to me tightly; but after leaving the group, she realized she didn't need me to find her way. The answer for her turned out to be that she needed to find her way on her own, without me or the group. In hearing this outcome, I knew that although it had been painful for everyone involved, it had been right for all of us. Everyone's virtues were honored.

**We all have sacred gifts as well as sacred virtues.**

**Sacred gifts are here to help you fulfill your purpose. Because they come so naturally to you, you likely don't even see them as a gift.**

**What is something that comes to you so naturally you may be overlooking its value?**

My personal sacred virtues are empowerment and faith. I beat up those kids in high school because I felt they were disempowering the people I cared about, and I couldn't take it. I stood up for my father because I couldn't bear to watch him being abused. In the story of our women's group, the woman I asked to leave had been disempowering everyone through her negativity and inability to contribute anything positive to the rest of the group. I could not continue to have all of us affected in that way.

Here's a sampling of virtues. For a better understanding of virtues and to understand what your virtue is, be sure to read *My Heart Virtue,* a book by Greg Mooers.

## List of Virtues:

| | |
|---|---|
| Compassion | Connection |
| Togetherness | Loyalty |
| Family | Community |
| Motherhood | Fatherhood |
| Righteousness | Integrity |
| Faith | Empowerment |
| Truth | Protection |
| Adventure | Unity |
| Peace | Hope |
| Love | Justice |

Once you discover your sacred virtue, you'll say, "No wonder I felt that way." A lot of things will begin to make sense. It's why certain situations hurt so much when they happen. The coolest thing about discovering your sacred virtue is that you can take ownership of what's important. Once you understand why you get angry or upset about someone or something, then you can ask yourself, "What can I do to validate my virtue instead of continue to let someone else violate it?"

## Sacred Wounds

Sacred wounds are caused when someone violates your sacred virtue. I always thought "No means no!" Unfortunately, my words didn't matter when I was physically taken advantage of at fifteen years old—it was a pure moment when I felt like all my power was taken away from me. When something or someone violates your sacred virtue, it becomes a sacred wound, similar to trauma that happens to you.

Sometimes the things that happen to us, that lead to sacred wounds, don't necessarily occur to hurt us intentionally. There are times when things happen to remind us of what is truly important to us, almost to the point that they wouldn't even be a memory at all or cause us pain if it weren't for our virtues being so important to us. So, your wounds can give you the insight you need to discover your sacred virtue. Once you realize your virtue, you can fulfill your purpose. When you are aware of your core beliefs and sacred virtue, you can then seek out how to make it your reality.

The events in my life of disempowerment, both in my childhood and as a young adult, have helped me see that empowerment is my virtue and remind me that this virtue continues to be important to me. Wanting to empower others, I constantly look for ways to offer it. Knowing this about me, someone said, "Faith, you should write a book," which was in alignment with my ultimate goal to let the entire world know I believe in them. And as I took more and more ownership of my purpose, events started to happen to help me fulfill my goal, including the writing of this book.

When you truly start to fulfill your sacred virtue, it happens without effort and doesn't have to be a struggle. Fulfilling your sacred virtue comes easily and effortlessly.

## Stepping Into Your Purpose

Once you realize what's important to you and begin to validate your virtues, you can start to assess life differently. If you are working in a job, you can look at it and see if it's violating or validating your virtue. For instance, if someone's virtue is compassion, they might volunteer somewhere that feeds homeless people. If someone is working in a position that doesn't validate their virtue, they may need to find employment that does.

If you aren't living in your virtue, you'll always feel like you want more. You won't feel fulfilled. You may feel like you are stuck or in a rut, or maybe at your wits end, because you are not doing what you are meant to do. Take action that is in alignment with that sacred virtue, even if you start out by taking on a hobby or volunteering at an organization that will allow you to fulfill that virtue. If your virtue is connection, join some groups so you can feel more connected. You get the point. Go where you are validated. Stay away from what violates you.

## Soulful Living in the Virtues

Once you reconnect to your virtues and your purpose, live from that place of soulful purpose. Fully be who you are meant to be and authentically live it, since your virtues and purpose have been there since you were born. Know and embrace those virtues in everything you do. That way other people can see who you are and what you stand for.

I truly believe that if everyone embraced their virtues and we could all make money doing what we love, we would all be taken care of. There are enough virtues for all of us to be happy doing what we love. We all have a place on this earth. We all have a purpose. We just need to soulfully see our virtues, live from them, and utilize them.

## Setting Your Purpose in Motion by Taking Action

Create and move forward with a plan to fulfill your virtues. Even if it's just one daily task, you can move closer and closer to your true purpose. If your sacred virtue is family, then start by putting yourself in places where you have the opportunity to be more family-oriented. Action is essential. You can use the Law of Attraction to create more in your life and manifest your purpose. Here are my simple steps to effectively use the principles of the Law of Attraction:

## Four Steps to the Law of Attraction

1. Ask
2. Be willing to receive
3. Take action
4. Don't worry about the how

Most people get caught up on #4—"how" they are going to fulfill their purpose. In my life, I want seven billion people to know I believe in them. If I had allowed myself to get caught up on the how, I never would have taken the first step. When you set your intention to move in the direction of your purpose, the how's will magically show up.

I was chatting with a friend and I shared my vision with her about speaking to a stadium full of 50,000 people. "If the opportunity arises, you will be ready," she replied. Most people spend their time looking for the opportunity before they take action. But none of us will be given what we can't handle. So, start taking the action and the opportunities will start to present themselves. Take action. Whether you make a phone call or meet a friend for coffee, do it today.

## Virtue Versus Victimhood

When you are really living in your virtue, it feels good. It's all connected to energy. When you are fulfilling your virtue the energy is so powerful you will attract more opportunities to recreate the same. However, if you are stuck in victimhood, it's impossible to live in your sacred virtues.

Someone who is living in their wounds is living in victimhood. If you haven't moved over from living in your sacred wounds to living in your sacred virtues, you are being a victim. People who are victims think that life happens to them, but the truth is, we have choices every single day. When you take ownership of your life instead of blame, you stop being a victim.

**The thing about your ego is if you let your ego win, you'll have you and your ego at the end of the day - which is a whole lot of nothing. If you let your ego lose and someone else win, you'll have a whole lot of something.**

When you are a victim, you often live in your ego and it drives you to make decisions. Instead, when you live soulfully, your virtue drives you to make decisions. Ego-based decisions leave you empty, whereas those decisions made from virtue leave you full.

I had a client whose virtue is truth. She had a need for people to stay true to their word. We were under contract on a house, and the deal fell through because the ad said "brand new appliances." The stickers were on the washer and dryer and they looked like they had come straight out of the box, yet when I went over to the house for the inspection, I saw the seller pull laundry out of the dryer. The seller's daughter, who was in college, had been doing laundry there during the time the house was listed.

Because of my fiduciary responsibility and understanding what was important to my client, I disclosed to her the fact that the dryer had been used. Her response was, "Faith, I wish you hadn't told me. This doesn't feel right." She ended up walking away and we found a different house for her. My client's virtue was violated, but because she was also living in a victim mentality, she expected people to lie to her. She'd had so many people disappoint her in the past that she expected the same result from others.

In the next transaction, when we were under contract, she felt the other agent wasn't being completely honest with us. I finally got to the root of the issue and assured her the other agent was staying true to their word. That's what she needed to hear. My client needed to be reassured. Unfortunately, because she continues to live in her wounds, in every circumstance she encounters, others continue to violate her virtue.

**Discover Someone Else's Virtues**

Use the favorite movie character question and listen for clues.

Ask them about a time they got so mad they had to walk out of the room.

She and I got along great because I recognized what was going on. I was able to be straightforward with her throughout our transactions, which was the only way we could make it work. If I had beat around the bush or not been able to be straightforward with her, our relationship wouldn't have worked. Since I knew what her virtue and her wound was, I was able to help her feel validated. Just by being aware of her virtue, I put her at ease. To honor her even more, I used words that validated her virtue by saying things such as, "Let me make sure they are being true to their word." "I'll follow up and ensure they are doing what they said."

A friend of mine relayed to me a conversation he had with his partner. He told me how he unknowingly and repeatedly said something to his partner that violated his partner's virtue. Whenever he would get mad at his partner, he'd threaten him by saying, "I'm out of here!" My friend continued to trigger his partner's core virtue. He didn't realize he was doing that, but he did know that his partner had a strong reaction each time, which was why my friend repeated this scene whenever he got angry. His partner's virtue is loyalty. When my friend finally realized he was violating his partner's virtue of loyalty, he started to change his language and instead said things like, "Let's figure this out together." Overnight, their relationship changed.

When you push someone's buttons you are intentionally violating someone's sacred virtue. Constantly ask yourself, "What am I doing to validate this individual's virtue?" You can use this technique with your clients, colleagues, friends, and family. We all want to feel validated. When you validate other people's virtues, they feel loved.

## Embrace Your Sacred Virtue, Purpose & Gifts

Ask powerful questions such as, "If I could fulfill my purpose, what would it look like?" "What action steps can I take right now to feed my purpose?" To answer that, we need to first look at our sacred gifts. Every person is born with sacred gifts that help them fulfill their purpose. When you use your sacred gifts, money comes easily and effortlessly—living is easier too. So, what are your sacred gifts? Well, what is easy for you? What came easy for you when you were in school? What took little or no effort for you to do back then?

We often think that work needs to be hard and take a lot of effort. That's a belief I learned in childhood—many of us, probably even most of us, did. As a result, when something is effortless, we think it's "not enough" or "not worthwhile." We think we have to struggle in order for "it" to be valuable. But…our gifts are easy because they are a part of us—and they are what lead us to our purpose.

My sacred gift is connection. I am able to easily and effortlessly connect other people, and this helps me fulfill my purpose. Often, people don't realize they have a sacred gift, but the second they discover it or recognize it, their world changes.

It's actually fun to recognize your sacred gift. Your gift is something you've done easily and effortlessly throughout your whole life. When you're using your sacred gift, people compliment you on it. Often, they'll say things like, "I wish I could do that." You probably think it's the most natural thing in the world to do. Yet for someone whose gift is different than yours, your gift will seem like something really amazing. Don't be fooled that because something comes easy, it doesn't have anything to do with your gift, your passion, and your purpose. Remember, your gift is easy and effortless—and always has been.

My friend Melissa and I were discussing how to discover her gift. She told me she'd always been good at reading maps and finding where places were. She'd gotten A's in geography. So, we identified that her sacred gift is navigation. Now that she knows what her gift is, she can find her passion around it and start doing something where she can utilize her gifts. Blessings will start showing up even more, now that she knows.

Once you identify your sacred gift, the next thing to do is ask, "How can I utilize this gift?" And then watch all the amazing things that begin to happen in your life.

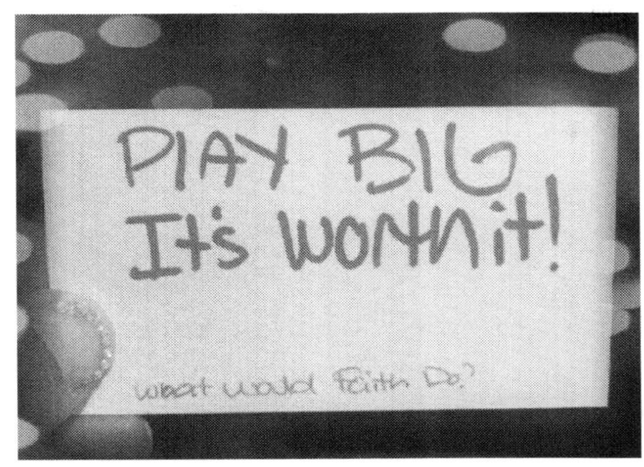


# Chapter 5: Living in Full Giftedness

When you are living in your full giftedness you are authentically being who you are meant to be. Your words match up with who you are, you act out of integrity, and when you are out of alignment you check yourself at the door. Your actions will always speak louder than words and show when you are living authentically in your full giftedness. Living in your full giftedness is also about playing big rather than being small. You have to show up fully.

Recently, I had an energy session with a friend of mine. I realized I had all this judgment about where I was going and who I was becoming. When I told people I wanted to write a book, a lot of judgment came out and I felt a lot of negative energy around it, so I wanted to do a clearing to release judgment, both my own and other people's.

One of the judgments that came up and needed to be released was from my older sister. From as far back as I can remember she has judged me. For example, when I was fifteen, I got pregnant. At the time, she was married and had been trying to have a baby for years. She was angry that I had been blessed with a pregnancy and she hadn't. The judgment directed at me from her, as well as from many other family members and friends, and even the judgment I held about what had happened, caused a lot of stress for me. I was overwhelmed and under a lot of pressure from both the internal and external negative energy, and ultimately, I suffered a miscarriage. It had been years, but I could still feel all this judgment directed at me from my sister. Last October she said to me, "I'm not like you. I'm not a real estate agent. I can't make $200,000 a year." I could still feel and sense that she was holding on to our differences.

**Make such a powerful shift in yourself that it causes a shift in someone else.**

In the clearing work I did, I released all judgment of who I am, where I am going, and what I'm supposed to do with my soul purpose. I realized that embracing my power and stepping into it was causing other people to be uncomfortable. We then released the judgments other people had of me and the judgments I had about them judging me. A few weeks later, my sister and I were at a social event where she introduced me as "the cool auntie." My mom and I looked at each other with confusion. Then, my sister proceeded to talk to me about my vision board and told me how she wanted to make one for herself. On top of that, two or three weeks later she interviewed for a new job, after being at the same job for twenty years. As a result of my clearing, my sister stopped judging me. It was amazing to see what happened when I did an energy clearing and how it also set her free. It was powerful.

## Playing Big or Playing Little

In the process, I discovered that I am no longer going to play little because playing little was a disservice to not only me, but also to my sister. The second I owned my full giftedness and embraced it I said, "I no longer accept your judgment." The change in me changed her life. When you embrace your power you are handed gifts that you never even knew were possible. When I embraced my power, I realized we are not meant to play little. Playing little no longer serves me. Because of this huge awareness, the possibilities are endless.

Sometimes, we just have to shift our awareness to a new reality or a new possibility. When a friend of mine told me what she wanted to do, I told her that because she was already doing that, she needed to dream bigger. Two years later, she came to me and said that I was right—she realized she needed to dream bigger. Within two months of proclaiming this, she landed a $12,000 client, all because she made the choice to no longer dream little. Instead, she decided to play big. How can you show up big in your own life?

## Be Ready for What You Wish For!

Once you get back to what you were meant to do and are doing what you are passionate about it, things start to happen to keep you on track. That's what happened to me when I was going through my divorce. The day my husband walked out on me, I had $6 in my checking account. I was a real estate agent and had zero houses under contract. I had a $600 car payment and a $1,200 mortgage.

As a survivor, I decided I'd do whatever it took, so I got a job within two weeks. I knew it was temporary, but I gave it my all. The job was 100% commission, and I worked my butt off. I decided that if I was going to work there, I was going to make money—and a lot of it.

Nine months after I started, I got written up for being late. I was a little shocked because I had been performing so well, but I kept plugging along. James Arthur Ray was coming to town, and I really wanted to hear him speak. I asked myself, "I'm scheduled from 11 to 8, and his event is at 6:00 p.m., so how am I going to get out of work?" I always say, "Be careful what you wish for." Well, by noon, I was fired. I thanked my boss that day. It had been a temporary job anyway, and by that time, I had three houses under contract and was ready to move on. The Universe had answered my prayers. Since I'd been fired, I knew exactly where I was going!

**Be careful what you wish for. Make sure it is something you really want.**

I went to see James Arthur Ray, and that event put

me on the path to where I am today. Because I was ready for more, the door opened and that opportunity was handed to me. Even though I wanted to quit my job and do real estate full-time, I wasn't quite ready to take that step and walk away on my own, so the Universe gave me the push I needed. The Universe gave me what I wasn't able to do for myself. When I walked out of my job the day I was fired, I realized I was going to be my own boss. I knew I would never work for anyone else again. I didn't care if I had to make 150 calls a day—I would do it for my dime, not someone else's. At that moment, I declared I would be willing to do whatever it took to work for myself. The cool thing is that today I only have to make 25 calls a day to be successful, not 150.

## The Universe Conspires In Your Favor

At the time I was going through my divorce and was at my rock bottom, I thought to myself, *How can it get any worse*? I was in such a negative place at that time that I actually did say this. And guess what happened? For a while, things did get worse. I've learned the hard way to be careful what you wish for. Today, I would never ask a question like this. I know now that I would attract more "worse" if I asked about "worse."

When you finally get in alignment with what you were meant to do, things start to line up. And when you discover what you are meant to do, the pieces fall into place, even though they may not seem like it at the time. Things may feel inconvenient, or you might hit a roadblock along the way, but all those seeming obstacles actually open up new paths for you to do what you were meant to do.

There is a beautiful story about Lisa Nichols from *The Secret* that portrays what can happen as the pieces come together. She had a dream of being on the Oprah show. In that dream, she saw herself getting up on stage and taking a seat on Oprah's couch. She could actually smell the couch in her vision. When her dream came true, and she was about to go out on Oprah's stage, to her surprise there were two stools waiting for her—but no couch. Can you imagine how she felt as she stepped into her dream to be on the Oprah show and realized it wasn't at all like she'd envisioned?

Her story doesn't end there, however. Once the show was over, the producers came up to her and asked if she'd ever thought about having her own show. Things were set in motion for that to happen and then she went out of town. When she came back, they asked her to come and take a look at what they'd put together for her set. When she arrived, she was excited to see her name spelled out in big lights. Then, she looked at the furniture they'd arranged, and guess what was sitting on the stage? Her couch! The exact one she'd envisioned! She ran up to it, sat down, and then realized it smelled exactly as it had in her vision.

I love this story because it's a beautiful reminder to not become disappointed when things don't seem to be working out the way you want. It may just be that the Universe has something even bigger and better in mind for you. Lisa Nichols' dream was to be on the Oprah show, but the Universe had something bigger in store for her. So, when something seems to knock you off track or doesn't turn out the way you think it should, maybe it's because something even better is on its way.

When you affirm what you want to do, things start to line up. When you tell the Universe what you really want and begin to take action, everything in your world begins to rearrange like pawns on a chess board. Know what you want, ask for it, but don't worry about the how.

Being career-minded, I always want to know the end result, but what if it's bigger than I've planned? What if I don't have to take the path that I see? What if the right path is not yet in my line of sight?

When I got into the real estate business, all I heard was how hard it would be, that it was going to be a lot of work. I thought to myself, *Hmm, it doesn't have to be hard for me. "Hard" can be everyone else's belief. Every other agent in Colorado can think it will be a lot of work, but that doesn't have to be my belief.* At the time I was still married. I came home and told my husband that I was going into real estate. He replied with, "What?! You are an idiot. This is the worst time ever to go into real estate." But I knew what I wanted and I knew where I was going, so I told him I'd be successful with or without his support. Turns out I became successful without him. I know that I am meant to do way more than work for someone else; I am here to empower the world.

## Fear Versus Love

When you are living in your ego, you are angry, you feel violated, and you feel like people are doing things to you. When you are living in your soul, you are at peace, you're loving, and you operate from your sacred virtues, not your sacred wounds.

Take, for example, a man driving down the road who receives severe road rage from another driver because he unintentionally cut the other driver off. What if the man's virtue is family or protection? He'd feel violated if another driver did something to threaten either of those virtues. And, if he is living from fear, he won't be in a space to operate from his virtues. Instead, he most likely would allow his emotions to control his response to the other driver rather than soulfully have enough awareness to say, "I violated something important to that driver by my actions, so let me send him some love so he knows I didn't mean to intentionally violate his virtue."

I had a friend who used to totally rub me the wrong way. She wanted to correct me for things I'd done differently than the way she thought I should have done them. She would call me out if I didn't do something she thought I should be doing, like include everyone in every event. I'd think, *Why does this gal rub me wrong most of time*? I finally asked her to tell me what her core beliefs were. Her reply: togetherness and inclusion. *Oh I get it now,* I thought. I then apologized to her for those times when I had violated her virtue. "Oh, that explains everything," I told her. "I'm sorry for any time I have ever made you or anyone else not feel included."

Since my virtue is empowerment, sometimes our two virtues didn't match up. She wanted to be sure everyone was included, and I wanted to include only those people who were ready to receive, who were ready to be empowered. I knew that sometimes I needed to empower others on a one-on-one basis, and including everyone didn't have the same effect. Yet, by me being my authentic self, I was violating her authentic self. As soon as I took a second to absorb this information about her, and was willing to step away from ego living, I asked myself, *What can I do to make her feel included*?

Once I realized what I'd done, I still did what I needed to do to honor my core belief, but I didn't get emotional about it anymore. I didn't need her to empower me, I realized. And I could empower her by showing her why I wasn't including everyone. I could take those occasions as opportunities to empower her, which fed my virtue and acknowledged hers.

When I looked back at what had gone on between us, I realized that my ego was showing up with her. In a way, she was violating my ego because she would call me out on things I was doing wrong. That was not empowering to me; it was disempowering. My ego would come up and get defensive. When I looked at this further, I realized my core belief was being violated, and although I knew it was important to not take things personally, it was hard not to. Wanting to live a soulful life, I quickly questioned, "How is this a reflection of me?"

When you switch out of ego and go into a soulful life and truly embrace those virtues, you start to recognize where your ego may still show up, or where other people's ego is showing up and how you can help back down their ego or take it out of an ego-based conversation. With my friend, after I understood what she needed to feel included, I made sure she was invited and I asked her to invite other people as well. I showed her grace and allowed her to continue to be in my world. She continued to show others they were included by inviting them and also came to understand where I was coming from.

## Where Are You Operating From —Fear or Love?

We can choose to live and operate from fear or love. Each and every day we get to choose. It is our choice on a daily basis. And the result of each will look completely different, including our experiences, depending on which one we choose. The good news is that every day is a new opportunity to make a new choice. Even if we chose fear yesterday, we can choose love today.

<u>INDICATORS OF FEAR</u>

Isolated
Passive
Arrogance
Self-Serving
Financial Scarcity
Controlling
Judgmental
Resisting Change
Instability
Scarcity
Competition
Critical
Expectations
Pessimistic
Aggressive
Inauthentic
Full of Doubt

<u>INDICATORS OF LOVE</u>

Connected
Expansive
Humility
Altruistic
Financially Secure
Allowing
Accepting
Embracing New Possibilities
Stability
Abundance
Inclusion
Expansive
Free of Expectations
Optimistic
Calm
Authentic
Faith

## Which One Will You Feed?

An Old Cherokee Tale of Two Wolves

*One evening an old Cherokee Indian told his grandson about a battle that goes on inside people. He said, "My son, the battle is between two 'wolves' inside us all. One is Evil. It is anger, envy, jealousy, sorrow, regret, greed, arrogance, self-pity, guilt, resentment, inferiority, lies, false pride, superiority, and ego.*

*"The other is Good. It is joy, peace, love, hope, serenity, humility, kindness, benevolence, empathy, generosity, truth, compassion and faith."*

*The grandson thought about it for a minute and then asked his grandfather, "Which wolf wins?"*

*The old Cherokee simply replied, "The one you feed."*

This is such a lovely story—so simple and yet so true. I think each and every one of us has these two wolves running around inside us. The Evil Wolf or the Good Wolf is fed daily by the choices we make with our thoughts. What you think about and dwell upon will in a sense appear in your life and influence your behavior.

We have a choice: feed the Good Wolf and it will show up in our character, habits, and behavior positively. Or feed the Evil Wolf and our whole world will turn negative—like poison, this will slowly eat away at our soul.

The crucial question is, "Which are you feeding today?"

# Chapter 6: Creating Space for What's Possible

## Managing Hidden Beliefs to Create Space

It's common for people to set goals and have a vision for their life. What I've learned in my own life, though, is that by setting goals and creating a vision, I was actually limiting myself. I remember when I started coaching with my life coach and I said these words, "This is going to be bigger than I can imagine."

Your thoughts can limit you. When people say, "I want to make a million dollars," I say back, "What if you have the possibility of making ten million?" Anything is possible if you don't limit yourself.

A gal who was in my women's group told me she was on a five-year plan. She said that she'd be making a certain amount of money in five years and would have a certain number of recruits in place to be successful. I looked at her and said, "FIVE YEARS? Are you kidding me? What if you could do that in five months?" Her mouth fell open with an expression similar to: *What? No one has ever said that before!* Sure enough, six months later, she walked across a stage as a director in her company. She came back to tell me about it. "Thank you for creating the space that I could do this in months instead of years," she said, "If it wasn't for you, I would still be on my five-year plan."

It's our hidden beliefs that will hold us back. Not just other people's beliefs about what we can do, but our own hidden beliefs about what we can or cannot create. My mom was a single mom and worked her butt off, because she held the belief that you had to work hard and nothing was ever handed to you. That thought became a hidden belief that stopped me from creating more in my own life. Man, are things completely different now that I got rid of that belief! I released the hidden belief that I have to work hard and that nothing will ever be handed to me. The second I switched it to, "Things come easily and effortlessly and I'm always taken care of," the coolest things began to pop up.

A good friend of mine recently shared with me how we all have defining moments in our lives. They are those pivotal points when we literally shift, like the way my car accident at age eighteen turned out to be a defining moment in mine. In my women's group, she shared that I had been a defining moment in her life when I started to coach her. She literally held so much belief that things have to come hard and everything is a struggle, that it was all she knew. Through our relationship, she's moved to a place where she no longer worries about the how. And she now has the most magnificent gifts coming into her life.

Here's just one example of how her life has transformed. She and I were talking, and she shared how she was struggling with money. I then told her the story of another friend, Leslie, who I was also coaching. Leslie was having trouble with her mortgage. I had asked Leslie, "What if you received $1,000 unexpectedly, would that change your attitude?" She agreed that it would and said it was exactly what she needed. "Awesome!" I said. "So, let's create some space for that and not worry about the how."

Seven days later she called me and said, "Faith, you won't believe it." *Of course I will,* I thought. She then told me how her mom had sent her a check for a $1,000 without Leslie even asking. *Of course she did! That's what happens when you don't worry about the how.* I said, "Leslie, I want you to remind yourself of this moment for the rest of your life. We created space for something you thought was impossible so that it could become possible. By allowing the possibility for something to happen and not worrying about the *how*, it did." It was magic!

I told my good friend this story to inspire her to allow space and not worry about the how. Two days later, one of her girlfriends said she wanted to meet her, as she had something for her. She met her friend, and her friend presented her with a $400 gift card to King Soopers. That amount represented enough money to buy food for her and her three kids for the next four weeks. Again, magic!

My friend decided to tell another friend when they were having lunch together. She shared with her the way blessings were coming into her life and how things were showing up for her, like the grocery gift card. Her friend asked what she could do for her. My friend thought of my story and how we can create opportunity for something bigger. She thought, *Well, let me just put it out there.*

"You know, I am having trouble paying my rent and it's due in three days."

"How much is your rent?" Her friend probed. "I'm going to write you a check right now." And her friend wrote a check for her rent right there on the spot.

What's so cool about this is that if I hadn't shared the story with my good friend about another friend, Leslie, she wouldn't have created the space to have $1,500 handed to her. It was simply because she allowed it and created the space. She also was willing to receive. And remember, she didn't ask her friend to pay the rent; she just told her she was having trouble paying it. When her friend offered, she received it graciously. We have to be willing to receive. Had she rejected the $400 gift card, there's no way the rent would have manifested. That's the most important thing to remember. One opening creates the possibility for more.

I was telling my coffee cup story to my women's group, which you'll hear more about later, asking them that if they reject a $3 cup of coffee, why would the Universe give them a thousand dollars. In rejecting $3, we are basically telling the Universe we don't need anything. We don't realize that we are all tied and connected to everything and everyone. If, for instance, you drop your briefcase and the papers go flying out because the case popped open, and then someone offers to help you pick them up and you refuse their help by saying something like, "No, I got it, I got it," it says to the Universe that you are not willing to receive and that you don't need any help.

**What's the story inside you?**

Most people are used to taking care of themselves, and in doing so, they often reject exactly what they need. So, an hour later, when they have a flat tire and no one shows up to help, it's more than likely because they have created a habit of rejecting help. Why would the Universe continue to offer you more help if you rejected it earlier? It won't. The Universe figures you don't need help now, since you just turned down the offer moments earlier. People don't realize that they are actually hindering themselves by turning away things, whether it's a cup of coffee or accepting help from someone to pick up their papers. Receive it all.

Believe it or not, right after I told that story to my group, as I walked out the door, I dropped my briefcase and my papers flew out. One of the women in the group rushed over and in her excitement said, "Let me help you! Let me help you!" She stated that the story had powerfully impacted her and she wanted to be there to give. "I'll receive your help graciously," I told her.

And…what had happened in that moment was a perfect example of, "what you think about you bring about." I had just spoken about dropping a briefcase and being able to receive help, and immediately following that conversation, they both happened to me.

## Releasing a Belief

With every belief you have, you need to ask whether it belongs to you or someone else. The belief I had about needing to work hard because nothing would be handed to me for free wasn't mine. It was what I had been taught by my mom. She was a workaholic, and for ten years she worked three jobs without one day off. That's what I was taught. That wasn't my belief—I just adapted to it. I thought that was the way it had to be.

Ask yourself, "Is this mine or is this someone else's?" And if it is not yours, you can release it easily by saying to yourself, "I'm going to give that back to them and I'm going to create my own belief now about how things come easily and effortlessly."

Giving a belief back to someone is simply a metaphor. When you recognize that it is someone else's belief and acknowledge that it no longer serves you, you release it. The belief is not a negative thing; it's just energy. Their belief is their "sentence," not yours. So you can send it back to them energetically by saying, "That's your sentence. Thank you, but no thank you." Energetically, you return it to them. You send it out and allow new energy and new space to come and eliminate what was already there. It's as if you cleanse yourself of that belief. You eliminate it out of your consciousness and your subconscious so it no longer dictates how you act.

If the belief is something you own, you need to switch your language. For example, rather than saying, "I am always late," which is a negative belief, change it to, "I am always on time." Whatever the belief, find a way to turn it into a positive form.

A recent belief in my life that I touched on earlier is, "Playing little no longer serves me." Even that sentence is rooted in negative belief, so what I say now is, "From now on, I will show up big" or "Showing up big serves me." It's the same idea, but stated in a positive form. Playing little was my own belief. Somehow this belief came to be in my life and I thought I needed to play little to protect other people. Since it no longer serves me, I switched it to a positive affirmation. You can do that with any of your own beliefs as well.

> I've had bling in my hair for almost three years. It's a hair extension—a long strand of tinsel. It's my signature thing. When strangers ask me about it, I say, "If you're going to show up, then show up big." It's not just with my hair and my bling—it's with everything. People meet me and I see them thinking, Huh, even her hair is showing up big.

## Creating Space to Create a Shift

Creating space in your life is simply shifting to a consciousness level of awareness to say something is possible without being concerned about how it will happen. Take my friend who needed $1,000 for her mortgage. She had no idea how she was going to pay her mortgage that month. You don't need to worry about the how.

People get too caught up in having the answer. When you take out the how, however, it creates awareness that something is now possible. Rather than worry about how something will happen, just imagine what it will feel like when it does. *The Secret* says you have to imagine the feeling to create what you want. If, for example, you want a Lamborghini, you've got to FEEL IT, hearing the sounds of its engine and the sensation of the steering wheel beneath your hands. The same is true for getting rid of a negative belief—feel the opposite of that negative belief, the feeling of what you DO want to create.

**You've got to feel it to receive it**

When you create space, it is not about having the answer. It's an openness to receive. It's creating actual space in your Universe for miracles to happen. Instead of a scarcity mind that says, "There's no way I'm going to get a thousand dollars—I'm going to be homeless next month," create space for what else is possible. With that being said, we're always taken care of.

## We're Always Taken Care Of

We're always taken care of, right? I say this all the time. I ask people if they've ever been homeless. Twice, I've had people say they've been homeless. Both times, I asked them if they had a car to sleep in. Both said yes. "You were taken care of then?" I questioned. They both agreed 100%. At the end of the day we're always taken care of—it's just a matter of our perspective on what it looks like to be taken care of.

Create space for bigger things to happen. Don't limit yourself. The only reason you don't have something right now is because you don't believe it's possible. So, ask yourself, "What can I shift to make it possible? What can I do to reaffirm to the Universe that I'm ready?"

## More on Fear

Fear—it's just like what you think about you bring about. Even dropping my briefcase that I mentioned before shows that I thought about it and then it happened. People think about and are afraid of what they don't want. I ask people what's their biggest fear? What's really sad is that the majority of people have an answer.

When my life coach asked me that same question two years ago, I said I didn't have one. He couldn't understand that. He said everyone has something they fear. But, because I'd already dealt with my biggest fear I no longer had one. That fear had come through during my divorce, and at that time I took ownership of it. Once I realized that I was in control of my life, I understood that there was no more need for me to be in fear.

My biggest fear had been abandonment. My father left when I was only fifteen years old. Without warning, I never saw him again. As you can imagine, I became afraid that people would leave me, especially people who loved me, and most especially, men. I constantly obsessed about my fear. I would say things to myself like, "Everyone leaves me," or I would say out loud, "Please don't leave me." Even in my marriage, I allowed myself to be victimized to avoid being alone.

Whatever you fear most tends to come true. The thing about fear is that it will dictate what you create in your life. Since my fear had been abandonment, it came true when my husband walked out of my life. My fear manifested completely. That was one of the most disempowering days of my life. When my husband walked out, I was left there by myself—completely disempowered—as if all my power had been ripped right out of me. I never wanted to recreate that pain again, so I shifted that fear to say, "I have more than enough people who love me and believe in me." I took ownership of my thoughts, and I let go of that fear of abandonment and shifted it to what I did want.

**What you fear, you bring near. The more it's a part of your thoughts, the more you'll create it in your life.**

What I do know is that I'll never be abandoned again, because I changed my belief about my own fear. Instead, for the rest of my entire life I will have people who love and support me.

When you put your fear into a positive form you can change what you are putting out there—your actions and those thoughts that you think about you bring about. Your fear is actually showing you what you really do want. You just need to change that fear into a positive form. It sounds easy, but it's true. Abandonment was mine, and even though I had evidence that it was a true fear, since my father left when I was fifteen, it didn't mean it had to be my life sentence. Instead, I switched it around. I now say, "I always have people who love and support me. I always have men in my life. I have people who love and believe in me every day. How does it get better than that?" I always say if you want more of something in your life (whatever that might be), be grateful for what you have in your life already. So, in my own life, I'm grateful for the friends and men who are in it now.

Use your calendar or alarms to remind you to state affirmations and beliefs in the positive. Here are a few of the alarms and reminders that I use for affirmations.

Think about your greatest fears and turn them into a positive, or what you do want.

I fear being homeless =
I am always taken care of.

I fear being alone =
I have love and support all around me.

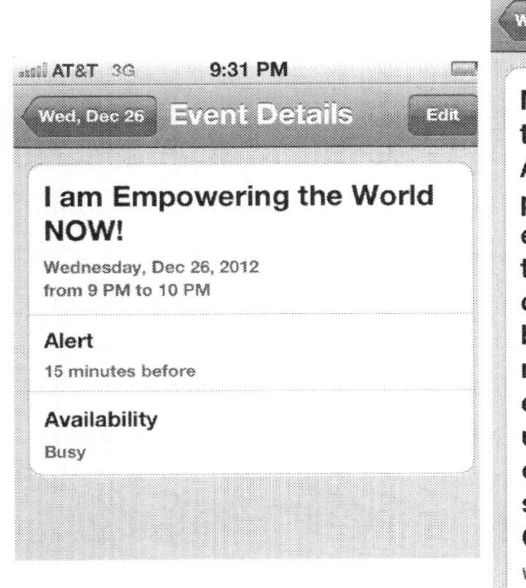
AT&T 3G 9:31 PM
Wed, Dec 26 Event Details Edit

**I am Empowering the World NOW!**

Wednesday, Dec 26, 2012
from 9 PM to 10 PM

**Alert**
15 minutes before

**Availability**
Busy

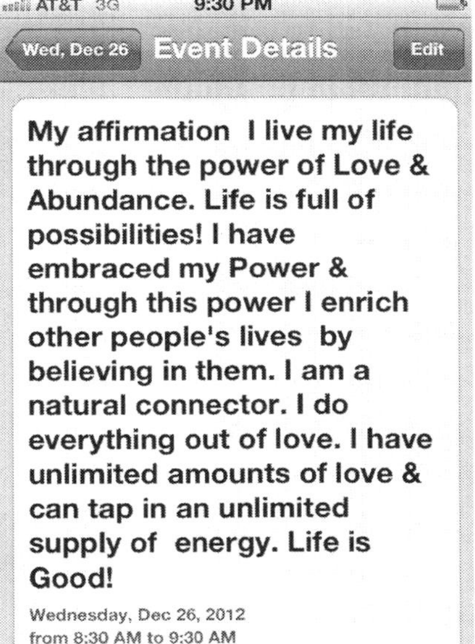
AT&T 3G 9:30 PM
Wed, Dec 26 Event Details Edit

**My affirmation I live my life through the power of Love & Abundance. Life is full of possibilities! I have embraced my Power & through this power I enrich other people's lives by believing in them. I am a natural connector. I do everything out of love. I have unlimited amounts of love & can tap in an unlimited supply of energy. Life is Good!**

Wednesday, Dec 26, 2012
from 8:30 AM to 9:30 AM

# Chapter 7: Understanding the Big Picture of the Universe

As I've said before, we are all connected.

The documentary film "I AM" portrays another significant event that took place on the day of the September 11th tragedy. The movie talks about number generators that are located throughout the world. These are little machines that spin numbers randomly all over the world each day, creating completely different numbers in each place. For example, the number in Texas might be 83446688 and in Rome, it would show up as 63241874. Normally, they generate numbers in a random, yet consistent manner—they've been doing this for decades. It may seem hard to grasp, but what hap-

The more loving I am the more significant I become.

pened to them on September 11th is a great example of the impact of our energy. When the towers fell, all the number machines went to 00000000...at the exact same time. While the world was focused on the horrific events of September 11th, the machines—which measure human consciousness, energy, and patterns—were impacted.

Our connection is way bigger than people imagine. We are all one in this world. We are all one being, and all energy is connected. More and more of us are beginning to understand and appreciate this. Our connection through energy is why when you are mean to someone it comes back to you tenfold. At the same time, when you offer love to others, it also comes back to you tenfold. The more love we give out, the more connected we realize we are, the more compassion we spread, the more gratitude we share, and the more all of these feelings will come back to us.

If we own and embrace our own energy, imagine what we can create. Whatever you do today is what you bring about for tomorrow. If you put out positive energy, positive energy comes back to you. It's all connected. What you put out you receive. When you give from your heart, the Universe will take care of you the next time you need it.

When my girlfriend was sick with pneumonia, I called and asked if someone was bringing her dinner. She said no and I told her I'd be right there. I offered my help from my heart. I've been shown over and over again that I receive those same offers of love whenever I need them. That's how our connection works. So...are you there when someone needs you? Next time you have the opportunity to help, I encourage you to step up and give it. Pay it forward!

## On Track versus Off Track

What a better way to tell you you're off track than to literally be knocked off track. I've been in thirteen car accidents during my life. I know that number is not by accident or by coincidence, and all of them weren't my fault. When people hear about my track record, they don't always want to ride in the car with me. But I know now that what these accidents really represented were signs that showed when I was off track. And now that I understand that, I've told the Universe to give me much smaller signs.

It was about four years ago, at the end of January, when I had my last accident and discovered this truth. I was driving down the highway and the traffic came to a stop. I had plenty of time to slow down, but the guy behind me didn't. He rear-ended me going 45 mph. We got off the highway immediately and exchanged information. This was my thirteenth car accident, and I knew how this worked! I got to my destination and realized I was hurt. I've had whiplash many times, so I knew exactly how it felt. I went to the ER an hour or so later. Ultimately, in order to be healed, I needed physical therapy and additional treatment. There I was, fifteen years after the rollover accident that changed my life and I finally asked myself, "Come on, Faith. What is this telling you?"

I realized that what I was doing, who I was dating,

and where I was going were not my path. They did not represent the right path that I was meant to be on. So, the Universe was saying, "You aren't listening. I'm giving you little signs, but you aren't paying attention." The guy I was dating was not the right guy. He just happened to be the one I was dating while I was going through my divorce. He had been great because he helped me through the divorce. But because things weren't necessarily meant to go any further, he was what I had been thinking about when I got rear-ended.

The Universe gives you signs. Right then and there I declared, "I'm listening. Please give me much smaller signs from now on." Now, I do get smaller signs—messages like a deal falling through, or someone not calling me back, or a person disrespecting me, or a speeding ticket, or even tripping on the sidewalk. Those are all little signs from the Universe to let me know I'm off track. That's why I have to listen to my intuition and go with my gut feeling. If I listen to those signs before a situation gets really big or out of control, I won't end up getting fired or in thirteen car accidents. Those things only happen to us when we aren't doing what we are meant to do.

Now when I have little feelings, little messages, like *I shouldn't drive tonight*, I listen to them. God knows that we get enough signs when we are off track, but when we are listening, we also get signs reminding us we are on track. When something has gone well, I know it was because I listened to my gut feeling. And because I listen, they now show up all the time, on a daily basis. The more you listen, the more they'll show up. If you aren't listening, why would the Universe continue to give you signs?

## What Are Signs?

Signs can be anything from tripping on a sidewalk to a car accident. Animals are known to have their own significant meanings, and each one represents a sign for something different. I see black ravens everywhere I go. A lot of people associate this animal with death. It's an old superstition. But instead of having a negative belief about ravens, I have a positive one. They tell me that we are never alone. I see it as a sign that my grandmother or guardian angel is watching over me.

A while ago, I went to my niece's graduation and had to park far away. As we walked toward the graduation ceremony, I looked up and saw a black raven. I got my sister Heather's attention and told her our grandmother was there with us. After the graduation, my niece felt sad and said she wished our grandmother had been there to see her graduate. I told her she had been, because I'd received the sign on the way in.

Whatever meaning you give to a sign—whether it comes through a bird, a feather, or a car accident—those meanings have significance. Listen to them. Embrace them. The spiritual meaning of a crow or raven is that they represent magic, and I see magic almost every day.

Later, after I declared what car accidents meant in my life, I headed to meet a client during rush hour. The car in front of me slowed down. Instantly, I felt myself go back into what I had recently learned and...*whoa!* I heard the sound of brakes behind me, and I cringed. *Oh please have enough time to stop,* I thought. He stopped in just enough time, but he was so close I couldn't see his headlights. Then the next person slammed into him. BAM, the next person slammed into him. BAM, the next person slammed into him, and BAM, the next person slammed into him. It was a four-car pile-up.

**When have you seen a sign that shows you are on track?**

When I got to my destination, I looked again to make sure the guy behind me hadn't hit me. It had been so close. He hadn't hit me, but it was surreal. At that moment I said, "Thank you Universe for reminding me I'm on track even if it was by just one inch. Apparently, the guy behind me was off track. You can be on track by just one inch, but still headed in the right direction. Thank you Universe for reminding me that I'm on track!" We might get reminders that we are off track, but the ones we get to remind us we are on track need to be taken in with gratitude. Embrace them, acknowledge them, and appreciate them.

# Chapter 8: Unlocking Gratitude

Gratitude happens on such a simple and basic level. Even the air we breathe is not something we are entitled to—it's a gift. Too many people think they are entitled to everything, and they see themselves as victims. If you clock in and clock out, you think you should get paid. Well, there's a lot you need to do in between clocking in and clocking out. And it's not about entitlement. Thinking you are entitled means you are living an entitlement role. And, if you are in entitlement, you are likely coming from fear and scarcity. No one owes you anything. Be grateful for what you have now, and only then will you receive more. The number one way to bring more into your life is to be grateful for what you already have.

My car had a cracked windshield, but I hadn't made

time to get it fixed. My assistant began to bug me about getting it replaced. I finally realized what that cracked windshield really represented. If I want to be authentic, and my windshield is an example of not seeing clearly, what is that saying about me? It's amazing how simple things like not taking care of a cracked windshield can affect other things.

Figuratively, a crack in the windshield does not align with seeing clearly or being able to see the future. Literally, while I am driving, it doesn't allow me to see very well. I realized that my windshield needed to be replaced so that I could have more clarity in all aspects of my life. Those things are connected. Will the Universe bring me a Lamborghini? Not if I'm not taking care of what I already have now. The more you take care of what you already have, the more the Universe will know you are ready to receive more.

Gratitude has changed me immensely. It helped me go from a negative life to a positive one. When I took my niece on a cruise before Christmas, I wanted her to see a glimpse of what life had to offer. I wanted her to know that life didn't have to be difficult or a struggle. What I wanted her to experience was way more than just the cruise. I wanted her to see that she could attract more than what she had in her life at that time. It gave her a new perspective on life and a sense of what else is possible.

When I came back on Christmas Day, I had $500 left in my account, and I wanted to get gifts for everyone. So I spent the remaining money on gifts. By New Year's, I didn't have any money left in my account. I decided then to ask my mom about the rest of my inheritance. My grandmother had passed away the year before, and I knew I had an additional amount coming from her.

I had spent $4,000 on the cruise with my niece, and just days later, on January 4th, the inheritance check came in for $7,500. *Thank you, Grandma!* That check reminded me that when you come from gratitude and know you are always taken care of, it will come back to you and it will be there when you need it. When you truly give without expectations you will always receive more than you give.

In *The Secret*, Rhonda Byrne wakes up every day and says, "Thank you" before she even gets out of bed. The more you are grateful, the more the Universe will give you in return. Even for the simple and most basic things in our life.

The best way to bring more into your life is to be grateful for what you have now. Every day, I write ten things I'm grateful for. On Facebook, as of Thanksgiving this past year, I'd posted for 730 days in a row what I'm grateful for. Because it's totally changed my life, I continue to do it daily. I didn't realize it could have this kind of power, but now people are seeing it and joining the movement as well—365 Days of Gratitude.

I was at a housewarming party last year for a client. The person who referred me was also there. We stood around chatting, when she said, "Do you guys want to know why I referred Faith to you, to be your real estate agent?"

I was thinking, *Yeah, I want to know. Tell me!*

"I know a lot of real estate agents, but the reason I

chose you, Faith, is because of your 365 Days of Gratitude," she told everyone in the room.

I had always posted "the little things"—gratitude for my health, the gas in my SUV—just those day-to-days that I was grateful for. Those little things landed me a $7,000 check from that referral. Who would have thought that posting those little things every day would generate something that big and tangible? As soon as she said that, I thought, *Damn right! I'm doing that every day for the next year. Imagine what next year will bring!*

What happens as a result of being grateful is not by accident or coincidence. People want to naturally help people who are grateful—people who spread light and joy. Now, I'm in Year Three of 365 Days of Gratitude and I have asked others to join me on Facebook. It's become a movement, a lifestyle, and a way of seeing the world and my life.

## Appreciation

If I didn't believe that gratitude would bring me more in my life, it probably wouldn't. If someone told me, "If I write that every day, it won't change my life," I would tell them they are right—it won't. They have just set themselves up for failure. How can it be a success if they set it up to fail?

The intention about gratitude is essential. Are you doing it for selfish reasons, expecting to receive more? Or are you expressing gratitude because you are genuinely grateful for what you have in your life at this very moment? If you are appreciative of what you already have, more will come into your life...but only if you believe it will. You set yourself up for success.

## Be Vulnerable to Receive

You need to allow yourself to be open and ready to receive. You need to be vulnerable. I allowed myself to be vulnerable so I could receive more love than I'd ever received in my life. I was at a three-day workshop with Greg Mooers. During one of the breaks, a gal asked me what vulnerability looked like and why anyone would want to allow themselves to be vulnerable.

I explained to her what it looked like for me. I used an example of how, when I'm having a rough time, I post on Facebook that I could use a little extra love. I allow myself to be vulnerable enough that people will send and receive this gift that I'm asking for. That's a form of vulnerability. I also said that I'd just made myself vulnerable by telling her my Facebook story to show her what it looked like. Then the craziest thing happened. She began to rattle off a list of questions.

"Well, do you even have any kids?" she asked.

"No."

"How about a husband?"

"I'm divorced."

"Maybe you're not even the right person to be talking to about this." And she walked away in mid-sentence. She left me there. As I stood there, I thought, *Wow! That was awesome*. I handed someone a gift and allowed myself to be so vulnerable that they could either love me or go straight for the jugular.

The next morning, I went up to her to talk about how she'd responded when she saw my vulnerability. I told her about my "aha" from our conversation. I had allowed myself to be vulnerable. I created some vulnerability in that space for her to be able to see it—not just for me to hear or tell her about it, but I created vulnerability in myself so she could actually experience it. I gave her a chance to love me or not. In this case, she did not.

Her response, "Yeah, exactly. So why the hell would you ever purposely set yourself up to get hurt?"

This left me even more enlightened. When our meeting started, Greg Mooers asked if anyone had an "aha" to share. I normally don't share, but I felt so compelled to share this with the entire group that I went up onstage. I started my share by saying, "I allow myself to be vulnerable so I can receive more love than I've ever received in my entire life." I continued and shared about my life, about negativity and scarcity, and how all of this caused trust issues and left me mainly living in fear. I finished the story by saying how much all of my experience was going to allow even more love into my life.

When I was done with my story, everyone in the room stood and cheered for me. I started to step off the stage and Greg wouldn't let me go. He said, "You might be done, but they are not. You need to receive your gift." People were yelling, screaming, and running to the stage. They were moved by my vulnerability. I then noticed the love they were giving me. I needed to move my body to receive it—to physically move. It was so intense, that I had my arms down by my side but I could hardly move them. So I did a little bit at a time, until finally, I was able to raise them above my head and spread out like an eagle in order to receive their love.

People said things like, "I love you" and "I'm so proud of you." It went on for what felt like ten or fifteen minutes. My heart was pounding. I received it all. I received exactly what I said in my opening statement, "I allow myself to be vulnerable so I can receive more love than I've ever received in my entire life."

It was such a natural high, that as soon as it happened, I wanted more. *How can I create more space to receive more of this*? My experience taught me that the reason some people don't have the love they want is that they don't allow themselves to be vulnerable and open enough to receive it. Just like the woman who went for the jugular. She had her walls up, blocking the love that was around her.

## Bring More to Receive More

One year, I woke up on Christmas Eve morning and knew I had a party to attend at a friend's house that night. I decided to check how much money was in my account. When I logged in to check it, I saw that there was an extra $500 in my account—money that I had written off as something I would never receive. It was awesome! What a gift! I had $500 more than I thought, so I decided to take that money and buy gifts for everyone who was going to the party. I got massages, wine, chocolates—enough items so that everyone there would receive a gift. That evening, we drew names and people picked out their gifts. It was really amazing.

I spent the night at my friend's, and the next morning she and I were pleasantly surprised to see two Christmas presents under the tree. Two of our other friends had left us gifts, but with everything going on we hadn't noticed them. We had both recently divorced, so Joyce and I were extremely excited and grateful. She had tears in her eyes, because she knew it was the only gift she would receive that day.

**If you genuinely give from the bottom of your heart, it comes back to you ten-fold.**

The night before I had given without any expectations, but it was such a treat to have a gift for me the next day too. Later on, I went to my family's house to celebrate Christmas. As I was headed there, I realized the gift I'd received in the morning might be my only gift that day too. In our family, we don't do gifts for the adults, just for the kids. But that year my mom had decided to give us all something. She handed me a card with a check in it for $1,000. When I saw it, I was practically in tears. *No way.* My mom had never done anything like this before. In the past, she might have given us $25 for Christmas, but that was it. I truly know in my heart that her gift was because I had given so much the day before. I received my gift back twofold the next day. If you genuinely give from the bottom of your heart, it can even come back to you tenfold.

It's like the Christmas cruise story. Just like the year I had $500 to give and I received $1,000 back, at the time of the Christmas cruise, I had $4,000 to give and I received $7,500 back. As they say, if you want to win big, you've got to play big. Not that the cruise was like a lotto ticket, but I gave without expectation. I wonder what I might create next Christmas? Can I give $25,000 away? When I have $25,000 show up on Christmas Eve, I will without a doubt give it away. Oprah's a prime example of how it all works—when you give without expecting, you receive because of it. She gives in such huge amounts that the Universe gives her more and more money in return. She's playing big.

Think about it. You can be grateful for lunch right now and by 6:00 p.m. you might have a free dinner. The simple, little things are easier to start with and appreciate. But consider some of the bigger things too. Gas in the car is a great one. My car takes $75 to fill up. Any time it costs under $75, I'm stoked! I posted that once on Facebook, "I'm grateful I got to fill up for under $75." Someone responded, "What? I complain when I put in $35." Put your life in perspective. My $75 gas tank is something she would have died over, yet it was something I was appreciative about. And my appreciation made her appreciate what she had too.

## Living in a Constant State of Gratitude

Switch your perspective to what is working rather than what is not working. Don't focus on what you don't have rather than what you do have. When you focus on what you don't have, it just brings less to you. Don't stress. All stress does is bring you more stuff to stress about. I always say that worrying just brings you more shit to worry about. The more thoughts you have about scarcity, the more scarcity you'll have.

A real estate client and friend complained, "That's how it always is for me. I always get the short end of the stick." She was referring to her contract and negotiation. I stopped her, "Sharmane, it may have been like that your entire life, but it doesn't have to be like that anymore. It can be easy and effortless. It doesn't have to be hard and difficult." She took a deep breath and said, "Okay!" She agreed in that moment that it didn't have to be hard and difficult anymore. Then, we got the contract settled.

**You can always use "at least" to get back to gratitude. At least... (fill in what you do still have).**

After that, all we needed was final approval for the loan. Once we were under contract, she handed me a thank you card and expressed her gratitude for how I'd helped her up to that point. The card read, "Thank you for helping me with this house hunting journey! It's in the underwriter's hands now. But no matter the results, I'm blessed you came into my life!" She made a positive shift in her life. I knew then that we'd close because she was able to appreciate what she had already.

The day of the closing, I called her. She said, "Are you calling me to say we aren't closing?" I assured her I was not and that everything was going well. "I just wanted to see how excited you were since we are closing," I told her. "Oh good," she said. "I threw some boxes at my son this morning and said, 'Hey, we are moving today no matter what, so start packing your room!'" She closed and she got her house. If I hadn't had the courage to tell her that it didn't have to be hard, so that she could allow the space for that transaction to be easier, it wouldn't have worked out.

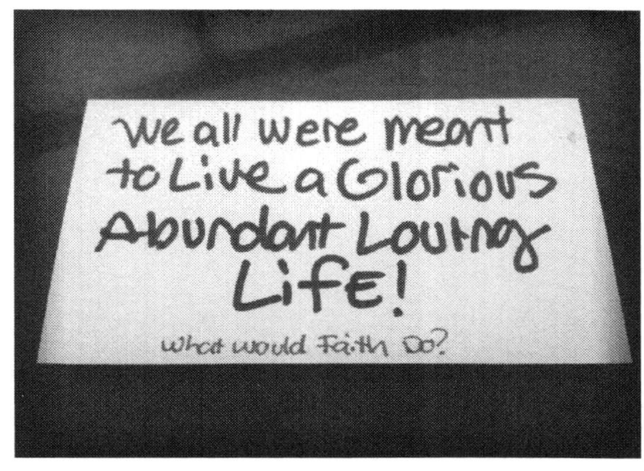

we all were meant
to Live a Glorious
Abundant Loving
Life!
What would Faith Do?


# Chapter 9:
# Living in Abundance

When it comes to being able to receive, I like to see where people are in their lives by offering them a cup of coffee. If they don't drink coffee or say no, I'll offer them something else. I do this because in a very simple way, it tells me if that person is ready to receive. If you reject a $3 cup of coffee, what else are you rejecting? I call it my coffee cup philosophy.

When you reject a $3 cup of coffee, you essentially tell the Universe that you don't need anything, that you are fine as you are. You don't need $1,000 or $10,000 because you can't receive $3. When you say no, whether it comes to a cup of coffee or receiving in another way, you block abundance from your life.

Something just as important, if not more so, is that you

are not only blocking yourself from receiving, but you also block others from giving. If I reject a $3 cup of coffee, it may be the only thing that person is able to give, and if I can't receive that from them, I'm hindering *them* from receiving more in their life because I wasn't able to receive.

It never feels good when you offer something to someone and it's rejected. Even if it is a glass of water, take the water. Receive something. Take one sip of it. That's all you have to do. Receive it enough to let the person know you appreciate them. Doing this allows them to create more abundance in their life. When you receive that $3 coffee cup, you'll also receive more in your life. You'll start to receive free lunches, free basketball tickets, free trips to Hawaii, or even $100,000, all because you are ready to receive.

I shared this philosophy with my good friend Christina Whelan when I first met her. We were at happy hour, drinking $2 glasses of wine. I offered to pay for hers, and at first she rejected it. I then shared my coffee cup philosophy. She was taken aback and so moved by my story, that she received the happy hour wine I bought her graciously.

About six months later, she had been practicing her coffee cup exercise when her son-in-law passed away tragically at forty years old. Christina's son-in-law's best friend called her and offered as a gift to the family to host the reception at his pub after the funeral. It was her son-in-law's favorite pub. He offered it at no cost. He said he would take care of everything. Christina practically fell over. There were about 300 people expected to attend the funeral services. She knew he was offering thousands of dollars in food and alcohol. Christina thought to herself, *What would Faith do? I have to receive this.* She knew that because this was such a large gift, she'd also have to convince her husband to be willing to receive. She did convince him, but in order to participate in receiving this gift of generosity, her husband offered to tip everyone. In the end, I'm sure the bartenders and staff all received his gesture graciously as well.

**Are you willing to receive**? If someone offers to buy you a cup of coffee, do you accept?

If not, you **are telling the Universe you don't want to receive.** Accept all gifts from others and then you also allow that other person the experience of giving to you. You stop the flow of energy when you say no.

At the reception, Christina spoke up and shared with everyone how the coffee cup philosophy shaped her life and allowed her to be open to receiving the beautiful reception they were enjoying in honor of her son-in-law. She then encouraged everyone there to go out and receive coffee from everyone who offered it.

The other beautiful part of this story is that her son-in-law's friend, who could not bring his friend back, was able to offer this gift from his heart to show his love and appreciation for his dear friend. What I know is that this gift would have never presented itself had Christina not been practicing receiving prior to that. And, at the same time, she gave wings to my story by sharing it that day with all those people. What another amazing gift to give.

When you see yourself saying no, you can then bring awareness to it so you can shift it. If you hear yourself saying no, shift that to, "You know what, yes, you can help with drying the dishes." If you find yourself in a situation where you reject someone's offer, see if there's an opportunity to receive it somehow. Reverse the thoughts immediately. It's a new way of thinking. Can you change overnight? Yes. But sometimes people have "I don't need anything" so engrained in their life that it may take some time to learn how to adjust to graciously receiving.

## Receive Graciously

If someone offers something that doesn't cost anything, from water to opening the door for you—receive it graciously. The more you receive those things, the more you'll receive other blessings in your life as well. This one principle has completely changed my life. I even have a girlfriend who wants to take me to Hawaii this year, as a gift to me. It's all because I have been practicing giving and receiving. What's crazy is that most people don't even know they are blocking themselves from receiving until they hear this story.

One of my friend's mothers always offers her leftovers to take home when my friend goes over to visit her mom. Her mom offers her something, whether it's grapefruit or almonds or some other food. And every time, my friend rejects it. I finally told her it would warm her mom's heart for her to receive those leftovers, even if she walked out of the house and handed them to another person on the street. "You don't have to eat them, just receive them," I told her. Slowly, my friend began to receive items from her mother. Whenever she receives something from her, her mom brightens up. With that, her relationship with her mom has been totally transformed.

About a year after she started receiving from her mom, my friend was trying to refinance her house to a lower interest rate. She was having trouble qualifying because of her 1099 income. To help her, her mom took out $200,000 from a line of credit and gave it to her daughter. I said to my friend, "You do realize this gift would never have come to fruition if you hadn't received those leftovers." Her mom gave her whatever she could—from leftovers to a financial gift. But would the financial part have come if she hadn't opened herself to receiving graciously before then? I think not.

## Giving Back or Paying Forward

We all want to be nurturing and help others, so if you can graciously give and help others without needing anything in return, someday someone will be there for you.

Through the years there have been a couple of friends to whom I have lent money. They were in dire straits and needed the money, so I was happy to give it to them. After a year had passed and they hadn't paid me back, I said to them that I highly recommended they do so. I'd already done my good deed and I knew I would continue to be rewarded by the Universe, but I explained to them that the Universe would continue to take away from them until they did the right thing and paid me back.

When it comes to borrowing and lending money, I'm not really attached to receiving it back. I have already given to the person graciously. One day if someone who I lent money to decides to write me a check for $1,000 it'll be icing on the cake and I'll receive it graciously in return. But if that person chooses to pay it forward, that would be okay with me as well.

If you need to ask for help and borrow money, it's important to do so. It's right to take care of yourself and ask for help. However, when the time comes that you can do it, be sure to pay it back or pay it forward. By doing so, you keep the action of giving and receiving in motion.

When I was going through my divorce, I had to swallow my pride and borrow money to pay for my attorney. It was $5,000, and they wanted it paid up front. I had helped other people out when they needed money, and I believed someone would be there when I needed it the most. It was the first time I ever asked my mom for something and the first time she was able to provide it. She lent me that money. I was taken care of when I needed it most, because I had been there when other people needed it.

People put so much belief in money, that it can destroy relationships, mainly because they think they are entitled to having it back. If you believe there is more than enough money to go around, when you need it, you'll be taken care of. When you really believe this, you probably won't even be in a position to need money, but maybe someone will give you a free trip or it will come back to you in other ways.

Unfortunately, a lot of people believe in "tit for tat." That's not how it works. If I scratch your back, you scratch mine—eliminate that belief, especially around money. In my women's group, I tell them they might give ten referrals to ten women. Then it'll be an eleventh person, totally unrelated, who might send that one person ten more referrals. That's how it works. Not tit for tat. The more you give, the more you receive—and not always from where you expect. Give what you can right now. You are always taken care of whether it's an $800 loft payment or a $10,000 Lamborghini payment.

We are all connected, all energy. It's not that the rich get richer and the poor get poorer. That's what people are taught. There's more than enough for everyone. The reason why someone might be a millionaire rather than someone else is because they believed it was possible. Belief is huge when it comes to money—everyone has the right to live an abundant life. It is our God-given birthright to live a prosperous life. Not just for your children to live a prosperous life, or your mom, sister, or best friend, but for everyone.

My friend Dale recently told me that if someone prays for you and something good happens to you, make sure you share it with that person who prayed for you. My mom prays for me daily. I called my mom to tell her that her prayers were being answered. I shared how I was appointed as the chairman of the Young Professionals Network. She was honored that I called. It isn't something I would normally share with her, yet she was so happy that she wanted to know more. She even said, "Let me get a pen. I want to write this down." It was that important to her.

You need to go back and tell people who have done good things for you that things are going well in your life. You hinder others if you don't share it. Silent gratitude doesn't do anyone any good. Appreciation is the number one way to bring more into your life.

Every year I mail about 1,500 Christmas cards. It takes me approximately forty to fifty hours to handwrite each and every one of those cards. I do it because people aren't doing it enough, in my opinion. I shared this with my grandmother a few years ago. "Grandma, I'm mailing out 1,500 cards for Christmas." Her mouth fell to the ground. I asked her, "How many did you receive?"

"Five," she said, "And, one's from you of course. One's from my accountant, and..."

Many people are not doing acts of appreciation, but we need to do it more than ever. At a time when so many people act from a sense of entitlement, it's important to remember that showing people we appreciate what they've done for us is critical. Show others that you appreciate them and their actions rather than behave as if you expected it. Doing this will fill your cup.

Last Christmas was when I took my niece on the Christmas cruise. We got back on Christmas night, and I had this moment of weakness. *Here's another Christmas where I'm still alone. I don't have a significant other to come home to.* I was not feeling good about life in that moment. "How can I shift this?" I questioned. "I bet there are checks in the mail!" I try not to check my mailbox until I think something of value is in it. I went to the mailbox and opened it. I hadn't been home in a week. To my amazement, there were fifty Christmas cards in there.

I came back to my place and I laid all the cards out. I started to cry and tears of joy ran down my face because so many people loved me and thought of me enough to send a card. People wrote letters, telling me how much of a positive influence I'd been in their life. People wrote pages to me. Right then, in that moment, a moment I thought was one of weakness, my emotions turned to pure gratitude because that's what I had given out. I had given love. I had sent love to all of them in the cards I sent. I'll remember that moment for the rest of my life.

Maybe one of the cards I had mailed went to someone who only received a few cards, but those cards might have made them feel just as good as I felt with the fifty I received. When you send Christmas cards without expectations, send them graciously. By sending cards to others, those who sent me a card powerfully impacted me in return. I didn't send my cards to get business or to receive anything in return. My only intention was to send others love and let people feel important. That's what was so cool—it came back tenfold, meaning that I received back five times as many as most other people found in their mailboxes. And those fifty I received helped me feel a tremendous amount of love. When you give graciously, it's ten times more powerful, loving, and abundant.

## Be Grateful for What You Have NOW!

People constantly talk about things that are going wrong in their life, whether in conversation or on Facebook. "Oh, my unemployment ran out." "My car just broke down." "My child support is late." It always seems to be something.

If you talk about everything that has been taken away from you, more will continue to be taken away. I've had friends say, "What else could possibly go wrong?" I tell them, "You better learn the lesson you were meant to learn, because it can get worse, especially if your words are putting that message out there."

Someone who is operating from a victim mode believes life happens to them. If you win a bottle of wine as a door prize, people like to take credit for that and say, "Look at what I manifested." But when they run out of gas or have a flat tire, they blame everyone else and refuse to take ownership of it. It's all tied together. You can't take ownership of the good things and blame something or someone else for the bad things.

This is where the paradigm shift will happen, by taking ownership of everything. When you come from abundance, every little thing is a gift. If you want more in your life, be grateful for what you have now. Even if you have hardly anything, there is always something to be grateful for—gas in your car, the air you are breathing. Being grateful for what you already have will attract more of what you want, instead of attracting more of what you don't want.

My best friend from high school said to me, "Faith, if

it wasn't for bad luck, I wouldn't have any luck at all." Well, that's all she'll ever receive. If you think all you have is bad luck, that's all you'll ever have. Luck is a mindset and it gets misinterpreted. Luck is only luck if you believe you are lucky. And good luck or bad luck represent whether you believe things will come to you or not. So, shift your thoughts in order that you attract abundance instead of scarcity. And rather than offer others "good luck," tell them "I wish you well." That's what I do.

After my divorce, when I was working to get back on my feet, at one point I had $2 to my name. I came up to a homeless person on the side of the road and I took out my $2. I gave him $1 and kept $1 for myself. I knew that in coming from abundance I will always be taken care of. If all I had was $1, that would have been different. I didn't give him all of my money. To me, $2 was abundance. So I gave him half, and I still had something left for me. It's the same as how 51% positive thinking is all you need. Start with what you have now.

Knowing that I am always taken care of, I handed him the dollar with pure gratitude, and he received it graciously. The very next day, I had $1,000 handed to me. It came back to me a thousand times greater than what I had left. That is how you can attract abundance, by truly being grateful and generous. Generosity is giving without expectation. And although by practicing generosity you don't expect anything in return, when you give big you'll receive big too.

My 365 Days of Gratitude challenge is all about that, it's about acknowledging something every day that I can be grateful for. Good things continue to come, because that is what I focus on every single day—the good things. People who are "victims," or coming from a fear mentality, think about all the stuff they don't have—and that's what they'll get more of.

Start today and be appreciative of all you have now. Join the movement: www.facebook.com/Jointhe-365DaysofGratitudeMovement.

## Abundant Thinkers Always Look for the Best

Whenever I am waiting for someone and a person is late, I take that time to send love. I was waiting for someone recently, and when she arrived she told me how she had just been in a car accident. I asked if she was okay, and she responded that she was.

"Awesome," I said, "at least you are okay."

As soon as you say those words "at least," it shifts people from being in a scarcity mode to abundance. There might be a ding in her car or she might have gotten a ticket, but *at least* she's okay. When I said that, her body language shifted completely. The entire conversation could have been about scarcity and loss had we not shifted the energy. Shifting the energy allowed us to both be in appreciation rather than view what had just happened from a place of loss.

You can use "at least" with people in all kinds of situations. If someone just lost their job, you can say, "*At least* you have a roof over your head," or "*At least* you still have a car to drive to interviews." If people are really in a scarcity mode, they won't like it when you say this to them, but they will shift. "You are right, we do have that" is the usual response.

A characteristic of someone who is a scarcity thinker is that they think in terms of negativity and lack. "I don't have enough time." "I don't have enough money." "I don't have a good enough job." "My car isn't the best car." "I am not good enough." "I don't have the skills or resources." People who think of abundance say things like, "I am grateful for the car I have right now," or "I am grateful for the gas in my car."

I met someone for coffee this week, and when we sat down the guy said he was really busy. I then told him if I were him, I wouldn't use the word busy. He thought busy was a good word. But if I were to send him clients, my instant thought would be that he wouldn't have enough time to take care of them. As an abundant thinker I say to myself, *I always have more than enough time for new clients. I always have more than enough time for people who are important to me*. You are still ready to receive when you say that rather than stating how busy you are. "Business is wonderful and I'm looking to help other people as well," is another one I use. Have you ever noticed that if someone is blessed, doing well, and wanting more—you automatically want to help them?

**If you want something, ask. Just put it out there. Best case scenario, you get what you ask for. Worst case scenario, nothing happens. But you will never get anything unless you ask.**

## Gifts Can Just Show Up

When you get out of your own way and stop allowing your ego to dictate what you do or don't want, or what you do or don't have, it's amazing what can shift. Gifts start showing up everywhere.

I'd been trying to teach my brother-in-law these principles for a while, but he hadn't been convinced. Six years ago, I asked my sister and brother-in-law what their dream house looked like. I told them we weren't there yet, but we would get there. Last year, though, I helped them buy their dream house. When we were writing the contract, I asked if there was anything that could make this deal even better. My brother-in-law said he'd love to have the pickup truck that was in the front yard. So, I asked for it. And (no surprise to me)...we got it. At closing when he was handed the keys for that truck, I asked, "Do you believe now?"

## Give to Give, Don't Give to Receive

A big scarcity thought is that if you give to someone, you will receive something in return. That thought goes against the Law of Attraction. You can't give and expect something in return. That is entitlement. Entitlement is a scarcity thought. We are not even entitled to the air we breathe. The air we breathe is a gift handed to us each and every day.

"Do you know how to appreciate life? When you get breast cancer not once, but twice? Believe me. Whatever you didn't learn the first time, you learn the second time." That's what my friend Jenny, married with two kids, said to me as she was battling breast cancer and going through chemo.

As she was driving to chemo one Friday morning, her husband was with her in the car, although he didn't usually go with her. Every Friday, there was a guy on the corner holding a sign that read: I need money for insulin. And every Friday, Jenny pulled out a hundred dollar bill and handed it to him. On this particular Friday, her husband saw her do it. "Oh my god, WHAT ARE YOU DOING? You have cancer and you're going through chemo! We don't have the money to give to someone else!"

She turned to him and said, "I give it to him every Friday."

He was pissed off and angry. "We need that money!"

Her response was, "He needs it, and I give it to him."

As they drove along, they stopped at a gas station to get gas. While she was there, she bought a lotto ticket. She scratched it and won $200. "Ha! See, we are always taken care of. I just gained an extra $100 back!" Jenny told him.

The next week, he went with her again. The man was standing there on the corner. Her husband said excitedly, "NO, let me give it to him!" He opened his wallet and gave the guy $100. Then, they went to the gas station again and he bought a lotto ticket. He didn't win. "What? This is rigged! I didn't win. I just lost a $100," he exclaimed.

If you give $100 to someone to get more money for yourself, it won't happen. It doesn't work that way. You can't give with expectation. You have to give freely without any expectation. When you give without expecting anything in return, the Universe rewards you. That idea puts things into perspective, because people usually think, *Sure, I'll give money if I'm going to get more in return.*

It's just like when I created my women's group. I knew it had to be free. It was all based around the Law of Attraction—the more you give, the more you receive. There are so many leads groups and networking groups that charge money to be a part of them. What I believe is that if you pay $500 for a leads group, those people walk in with thoughts of entitlement. Many people think to themselves, *I just paid 500 bucks for this group; I better pick up some business!* To think you are entitled to anything is based in scarcity. The reason I don't charge a fee is that everyone then comes in with abundance. So, everything else that happens is icing on the cake.

Recently, I totaled the numbers from my leads group for 2012. I had given 300 referrals (warm introductions) for the year. This is a great example of how the Law of Attraction works. I gave them without expectations, and in return, I closed six deals from the group, totaling $28,250 in sales for the year. That represented 30% of my business from fifteen women.

You don't give someone a dollar and the next day they give you a dollar back. But so many people are caught up in that. If you give without expectations, you are always taken care of. That's the affirmation you should be saying about money.

If you say, "All I want is enough money to pay my

bills," that's all you will have—bills and just enough to cover them. Choose your words carefully. I repeat to myself all the time, "I'm always taken care of."

## You're Always Taken Care Of

Money is energy. When you store money in the bank for a rainy day, that's what's going to happen—a rainy day will come along. When you truly believe you will be taken care of, you'll always be taken care of and you'll always have enough money. Money comes when you need it.

I remember when a friend of mine was looking to buy a house and asked to borrow money from her dad for the investment. Her dad wouldn't touch the money he had saved. He said, "That's all the money I have." And, that's all the money he'll ever have. He could have doubled his money and then had a million dollars.

I haven't used a credit card in over six years. When someone asks me to do something, I wait until I can pay cash for it before I do it. People find it crazy when I say I don't have a credit card. They always want to know what happens in an emergency. "I'm always taken care of," I tell them.

For instance, I had an emergency with my puppy, Boo Boo, a couple of years ago. The vet bill was $2,200. I'd had a closing a few days earlier and had more than enough money to pay for that vet bill. That's how money as energy works. When you believe there is more than enough money, when you need that money, it will always appear.

Sometimes you might have to ask for it, though. My dog, Buddy, had bone cancer that I believe came about because of the state I was in after my divorce. Because energy is so powerful, my dog could feel my pain and he created physical pain himself. One day, neither he nor I could take his pain anymore. I had to put him down. I didn't have any money for it, and I really wanted the vet to come to my home to do it. I also wanted to be able to cremate him and have an urn of his ashes. In a dire situation and heartbroken, I called my mom. She said she would pay to have him cremated. It was such a miracle and a relief. The vet came to my house and laid him to rest. It was a peaceful experience for him and me. To this day, I have his ashes. I only have them because I had the courage and the strength to ask for help when I needed it.

**"There's enough energy in the world, enough abundance in the world, enough money in the world... and money, is just a form of energy."**
**- Marie Forleo**

I recently reminded my mom again how thankful I was that she did that for me and how much I appreciated her for that act of kindness.

## Knowing & Believing In Your Value

In real estate, when I list a house I charge a certain percentage. People sometimes challenge me on it. I don't blame them. I'm a sales person. I'd challenge me too. People will ask, "This other agent will do it for 1% less, so why won't you?" And I say these words in response,

"I have eight listings, and all of them are at the same percentage. If I take yours at 1% less than the rest, whose house am I going to work harder to sell? Yours or the ones I'll make more money from?" People usually say, "Okay, alright. Good point."

**If you're not using your gifts, it is stealing from the people who need it the most.**

The second thing I tell them is that I don't blame them for asking—I would too. My value exceeds what I am charging, and if those agents are willing to take 1% less after a five-minute conversation and lower their own bread and butter that fast, how fast do you think they are going to lower the price of your house when they go to negotiate with the other agent? Besides, if you get your agent to lower their commission, guess what you just did? You just outsold your salesperson! What do you think the other agent will do to them as well? When it comes time to go to bat for my clients, I'm going to bat for them, especially compared to that agent who buckled so easily.

The most important thing is that I know how much value I bring, so much so that I could charge even more. That's why I receive my full commission every single time. What's so important about value, which is completely tied to money, is that if you don't believe you are valuable, you will only make as much money as you think you are worth. If you think you are worth $7.50 an hour, that's how much you'll make. I realized that I used to have such limited thinking about what I was worth that I limited what I received. Once I understood that I was holding myself back, not only did I change what I believed but also what I said. Whatever I'm contemplating, whatever my intention, I always state that "it's bigger than I can even imagine."

Even our imagination can be a limited belief. It's all geared to what you think is possible. You need to create space for something even bigger than what you believe is possible. *It's bigger than you can imagine!* That's exactly how this book manifested. When I started coaching with my life coach I said, "This is going to be bigger than I can imagine." I had never fathomed writing a book. As a matter of fact, because I have dyslexia and graduated high school with a fifth grade reading level, I didn't believe I could write a book—it was not in my realm of possibility. This book has come to fruition purely because I allowed myself to think that something bigger was possible for me, a girl with dyslexia. I have thought big and here I am now. And who knows where all of this will take me? It's bigger than I can even imagine!!

## Give What You Want

I always share with people that I believe in them. It's what I want most to hear from others. As I was listening to Greg Mooers' program "Heart Virtue" in my car, he said, "If you want more of something in your life, give more of it. So pick up the phone, call someone, and tell them that YOU BELIEVE IN THEM." I literally, ERRRRRR, yanked the wheel and pulled over. I hit the back button on the CD to listen to what he said again. At that very moment, I realized for the first time why I was telling everyone I believed in them—it was because I wanted someone to believe in me.

It's beyond powerful, as now I have thousands of people who believe in me. When you are consciously aware of what you want, it increases tenfold. If you are going to show up, you might as well show up big. When you realize why you are doing something, it gives it so much more power to create more. If you want someone to love you, give more love to other people. If you want someone to send you good morning texts, send good morning texts yourself. It's one of the laws of the Universe, the natural law of reciprocity. In my life, I give words of affirmation to people all the time. When I tell people they are important, it feeds people's souls. And in return, it feeds mine.

## Sabotaging Abundance

A year ago, I decided I wanted to take a girlfriend to Hawaii. I had some abundance and unexpected income come into my life, and I thought it would be fun to take a trip to Hawaii with a friend. When I offered it to her, she got really excited and was practically in tears. Then, I saw something shift. I could tell that something was wrong. I asked her if I needed to take back my gift. Her self-worth was so low that she believed she didn't deserve the trip. I asked her, "Would you feel more comfortable if I took this back? Would you feel better if we didn't go?" She said yes.

I took back the gift and instead took my eighteen-year-old niece on a seven-day Christmas cruise, which

I realized was actually what was meant to happen. But what I also realized was how my friend was sabotaging herself and any good that was coming to her. If you think about the coffee cup philosophy, she didn't just reject $3—she rejected a $4,000 trip. And after that, she went into a downward spiral. She lost her apartment and her car exploded. I believe all of this stuff happened because she clearly told the Universe she wasn't worthy. People will sabotage themselves from good because they truly don't believe they deserve it.

## Your Worth

Embrace your gifts and what your value is. I make twenty-five calls a day so I can stay self-employed and not work for anyone else. When I tell people what I do, their usual response is, "Well, what do you say? I don't want to sound like a salesperson." Just those comments alone come from scarcity mentality and a lack of self-confidence. Personally, I can't even possibly make enough phone calls each day, because that's how much value I bring. I believe I bring enough value that I'm actually hindering people from receiving value by not making a phone call. Those people who say they don't know what to say, or state that they'll feel like a salesperson, need to reevaluate what they are offering and what they bring to the table.

I remember a gal who was in a multi-level marketing business, and she had a product I wanted to buy. She was in such scarcity mode that when I told her I wanted to buy from her, she never even followed up with me to place my order or take my money. She wasn't listening to the signs of the value that she could bring to others.

## How You Perceive Yourself

People will perceive your value based on how much value you perceive in yourself. If you only think you are worthy of $10 an hour, you can ask for more money, but that other person is going to see that you are only worth $10. If you want more in your life, believe that you deserve it—believe in your value.

We all deserve abundance and deserve to have more. The way you come across and show up is how people are going to determine your value. When those other agents said they would take 1% less, they were coming from scarcity. They were thinking, "Well, 1% less is better than zero or not getting the listing at all." When I have eight listings, I'm not coming from scarcity. Period. I've walked away from listings when people won't pay my value. If you are constantly trying to lowball people or use coupons, you'll attract those same kinds of coupon-type-people.

I was holding a jewelry party at my house and invited a friend who told me she didn't have money to buy any jewelry. She was in her own MLM business, similar to the one I was hosting, but sold a different product. I responded by telling her I didn't ask her to buy anything, just to come and support me. To get out of scarcity, you can say to yourself, "Who do I know who would want to buy jewelry? Let me invite them." If you are in your own business and you say you don't want to go to another party because you don't have any money to buy jewelry, guess who's going to show up at your party when you hold one? The same kind of person.

But if you are thinking outside the box and contemplating, *How can I support Faith and her jewelry party*? then the person hosting and coordinating a party for you will do the same. I know people can easily relate to this scenario. Have you ever hosted a party where people said they couldn't buy anything? The second people say, "I don't have any money," say back to them, "You are right, you don't! What you are putting out there is what is coming back."

Work on your own belief of what you think you deserve. The best way to do that is when you see that someone else's self-worth is less than what they are bringing to the table, work on bringing it up. Don't say things like, "Why are you with that person? Why are you at that job? You are only making how much money?" Instead, help them see their value and say things like, "You deserve so much more than that." "I love it when you are happy." "I can't wait until you make more money."

How do you help someone in this negative state of mind? By being a shining example. For instance, if you want your sister to date men that respect her, you better be sure you have respectful people in your life. Make such a powerful shift in your own life that it forces other people to shift theirs.

## Living in a Constant State of Gratitude and Appreciation

Every single morning I do my F.U.E.L. book, which was written by my friend, Trish Moore. F.U.E.L. stands for focused unlimited extraordinary life. The book is a journal where you write your daily intentions, ten things you are grateful for, your accomplishments and successes, and ten things you want. It helps me set up my day intentionally and not by accident. I start every day writing ten things I am grateful for. My assistant and I go over the F.U.E.L. process together— I tell them to her and she writes them down. Many days, I even have her write her own name as someone I am thankful for. She always appreciates that. Letting someone know is more important than even writing it, as the more appreciative you are about someone else, the more they'll want to give. It's the natural law of reciprocity at work. They feel good in the process and as a result they want to give more.

We all want to feel appreciated. It's a universal desire. If you manage people or have your own company, let them know how much you appreciate them. They will do anything as long as they know they are appreciated. The more you show appreciation for others, the more appreciation people will show for you.

I see appreciation come up a lot in marriages. Think about it. When a couple is married, the wife is always asking, "When are you taking out the trash!? It needs to be taken out." Instead, you can focus on when he does take the trash out by recognizing it and appreciating it. When you do that, you'll have to ask less and less. It's the

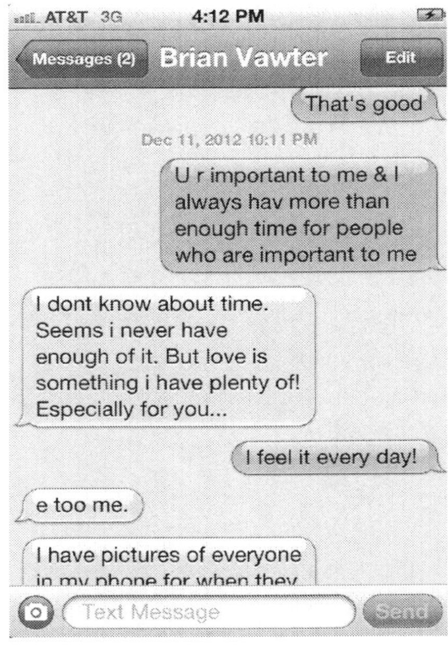


same if you cook dinner every night and no one tells you thank you. If you cook dinner for someone every single night and they never say thank you, eventually you will stop making dinner altogether. One day you are going to crack and say, "I'm not cooking dinner anymore!"

When I was married, I waited until my husband got home at night to have dinner. I thought that was what we were supposed to do, and it was how I thought I could show I cared. When my husband got home, he'd go into his cave and come out an hour later. By then, I was starving. If he would've just said thank you for waiting for him, I would have wanted to do it willingly. Instead, having to wait for him made me angry.

When you don't feel appreciated, you feel like you are sacrificing, which causes the feeling of resentment. Once you feel resentment, it's very difficult to reverse that feeling. Always appreciate people, even for the little things. Say something as simple as, "Thank you for taking an hour with me. Thank you for your time. You are important to me. I always have more than enough time for people who are important in my life." They will appreciate being appreciated.

## Setting Yourself up Every Day with Gratitude and Intentions

With my F.U.E.L. journal, I set my intentions for my day, every day. Here's an example of what I wrote recently: Find a buyer for a listing; pick up a new client on floor; get paperwork for closing; get approved HUD; have a successful closing on Victor; new client short sale approved on the ninth, have an enjoyable lunch with my friend. All of it happened that day. So, on my successes the next day, I wrote the same exact list. Those all came true because I set my intention for them to happen.

Too many people stumble through their days without having any real intentions or direction. They get up on the wrong side of the bed and then their whole day is off track. Setting your intentions every morning is one of the most powerful things you can do to bring more abundance to your life. Things don't happen by accident. I had sent the short sale to the bank four months earlier to be approved. Then, it happened on the precise day that I wrote it down. Sure, I may have written it down a few more times before that day, but it wasn't by accident that we got the short sale that day. Think big. Recognize it as a success. Then, you'll want to do it again the next day and the next.

When you write an intention and it comes true, recognize it. Celebrate it. Then, in the future, more and more things will come true. Little things at first, like a free cup of coffee. One day, I wrote on there that my intention was to get a free lunch. My assistant didn't believe it would happen. She said, "It's 11:00 a.m. How are we going to make that happen?" Well, little did she know that half an hour later, my broker swung by my office and said, "Hey Faith, there's free food in the kitchen if anyone wants lunch." See, it only took thirty-five minutes to manifest that one. It is fun. It's like a game. Easy and effortless. If you can manifest free lunch, start with that. Next, hockey game tickets, then Hawaii, and then $10,000 checks. And that's just the beginning!

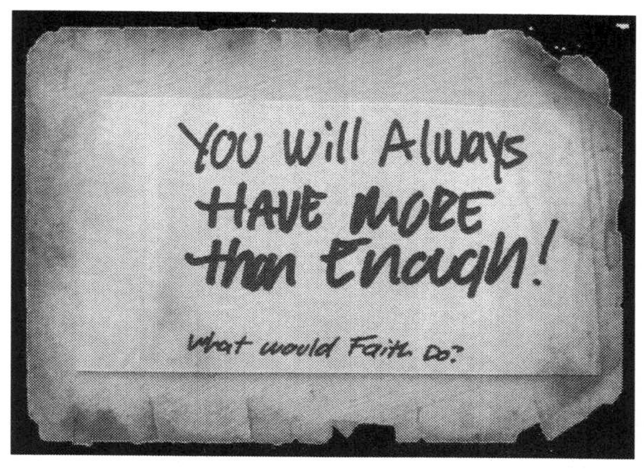

You will Always
HAVE MORE
than Enough!
What would Faith Do?


# Chapter 10: Manifesting Money

We all have beliefs about money—whether we grew up being taught certain things about it or we've bought into certain ideas as we've gone through life. Our beliefs about money, though, are usually what hold us back and keep us playing small and living out of scarcity. To truly have more in your life, you've got to change the way you think, feel, and act about money.

## Knowing Where the Money Comes From

What if you could just double your income? *Well, I can't get a raise. They'll never pay me that at work.* This is what people automatically think. But, what if you could get money from somewhere else? It doesn't have to come from your job. Even that idea is hard for people to grasp. People usually need to know where the money is coming from, but that's people's biggest downfall. It keeps the money from flowing. So, don't worry about the how. The Universe doesn't put value on money or how it will arrive—we do.

## Money Doesn't Have to Come From Your JOB

One common belief about money is that it has to come from your job. I see this with both entrepreneurs and employees. Believing that money can only come from your place of employment is a limitation.

A friend of mine, who was a part of my women's group, had the opportunity to give another woman a huge gift. The gift was more than the receiver could have asked for or received through her work, but my friend was able to give it when she chose to attend school in Rome for her master's degree. She had a houseful of stuff and decided to give it all away before she moved. The only things she kept were pieces that held a special meaning to her.

The other woman was going through a divorce and in the process of getting her own place. She didn't have any furnishings or household items but was determined to get out of the relationship and start over. My friend gave her everything—her bed, sheets, comforter, even her Christmas tree. Everything she gave her represented an invaluable gift that wasn't in the form of dollars, but if the woman had had to purchase all the things she received, she would have spent more than $5,000. People believe that in order to count, money has to show up in the form of cash or checks—the tangible representation of money—but receiving gifts like this, or a free coffee or a lunch, are all money coming your way. In this instance, my friend gave without expectations and you better believe she received in return.

The main point here is that money can show up anywhere and everywhere, as long as you don't worry about the how. Stop asking, "Where will the money come from? How will I be taken care of?" If you are thinking about your limits, you'll only experience limitations around you.

Two years ago, I wrote on my vision board "Unexpected income of $25,000." That year, I received three different sums of money that equaled almost exactly $25,000. The first amount of money showed up in an envelope with cash from my grandmother. The envelope was so thick; you couldn't even fold it in half. It was $5,000 in dollar bills. If you've ever held $5,000 cash in your hands, it's a lot of dollar bills! I had helped my grandmother, and in return, she gave me this gift. I, of course, received it graciously.

The second check arrived as the settlement from an accident I had been in the year before. Without any effort, I received it. It had been offered to me and totaled about $8,000. The third sum of money came to me in the form of a commission. I was working with a client who wanted me to act a certain way during the negotiations and the transaction. She actually asked me, in her own words, to "stop being nice and to start acting like a bitch." Everyone else was acting that way, but I didn't

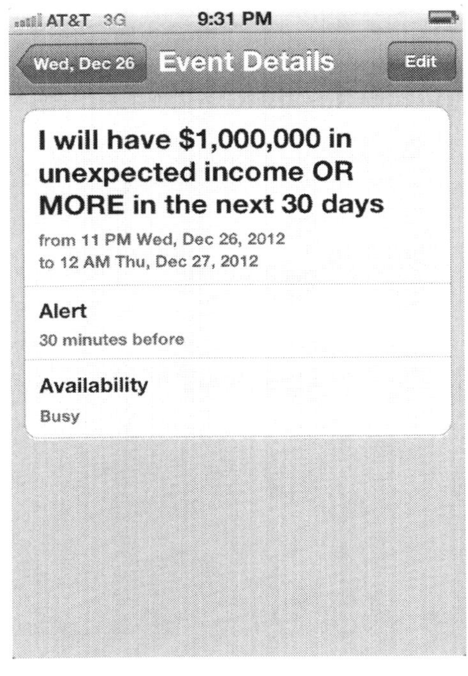


want to sacrifice my values to accommodate her or anyone else. My boss at the time even suggested that perhaps I needed to be more firm with people and that my "everything will work out attitude" might be coming off like I didn't really care.

I refused to change in order to be in the real estate business. If I needed to be someone else to succeed in this business, I'd rather go and do something else. Unfortunately, my client didn't appreciate my values and fired me for not portraying the bitchy person she thought I should be. This was the first and only time I have ever been fired by a client, and believe me, it didn't feel good. Instead of feeling resentful, however, I sent my client lots of love, and the most amazing thing happened. Since I was technically fired by my client, I wasn't owed the commission, but I still got a commission check in the sum of $12,000. It came in on December 28th that year. It was an amazing symbol to me that when I stay true to myself, it will all work out. I didn't need to change or become someone else in order to receive money.

After that manifested, I thought, with a bit of humor,

"Imagine if had put $250,000 on my vision board," but to me that would not have been reachable or realistic at that moment in time. You have to make it a realistic goal, most especially, one that you can believe in yourself. This year, I have $250,000+ on my vision board. It's time and I'm ready!

## You Are Worth It

People believe that if you have money you are selfish, but look at Oprah. She's a great example of someone who is wealthy and completely selfless. I truly believe there is more than enough to go around. Some people believe they are worth it more than others do. A previous assistant of mine—from a time before I got into real estate—told me, "You are the best sales person I know. You should make the biggest commissions!" *Huh*, I thought, *that's a good idea*. Self-worth is very important when it comes to money.

One month later, I had my annual review. My boss said, "Here's your raise, and just so you know, you are capped out. You'll never make more money in this position." That was a stupid thing to tell me. No matter how hard or how little I worked, that would be it? I decided in that moment that no one would ever tell me what I was worth besides me. That's when I got my real estate license and became a realtor. Ever since that day, guess who tells me what I'm worth? Me. I walk away from deals where someone wants to pay me less than my full commission. I can do this because I know that the value I bring is worth more. Just as I described earlier, if I get a paycheck for 1% less than what my other clients are paying, that deal won't be worth it to me. I want to work with people who see my value and who value my work.

A friend said to me once, "I just need to make enough to pay my bills." I asked her, "What if you could have more?" She was uncomfortable with that, so I proposed that she work half the amount of time for that same amount of money. She said she'd be okay with that scenario, since it would still give her the amount of money she needed to cover her bills. She was satisfied with that arrangement.

People usually think they can only have enough money to sustain where they are already—otherwise they think they're being greedy. It's not greed to want more, though, because there's more than enough to go around. The people who believe there's more than enough are the ones who see more abundance in their lives. What we believe is possible—and if we believe we deserve it—is what we will create.

We all believe we are worth a certain amount of money, because someone told us that at some point. If you are getting paid $10 an hour, that's all you think you are worth. Until you say you want more, you won't get more. You are paid precisely the amount of money that you think represents your value. I know that's hard to hear, but it's the truth. If you truly believe you deserve more, more will come. It doesn't just have to come in the form of your paycheck either. It can come in so many different forms—gifts, cash, inheritance, an increase in stock prices.

There are other ways we demonstrate our self-worth, or lack of it. For instance, have you ever passed up a front row parking space so someone else could have it? By doing that, you're saying you aren't good enough for the front row. When your actions say that someone else is more deserving of something as small as a parking spot, why would you be deserving of a large raise?

Recently, I was recognized as one of the top agents in my office, because I had twenty-one closings this past year. To put that into perspective, an average realtor does three transactions a year. The top 10% do ten transactions a year. I did twenty-one. My employing broker went through my stats for the year and found that my average commission rate was above everyone else's average as well. She said to me, "Faith, this is amazing. Only 5% of the office earns that much money. Most take a lower commission." I was shocked. For something I thought everyone should be doing, she told me only 5% of the agents in the office were actually doing it. I deserve even more than that, I thought.

If you want more in your life, go for it. Don't wait for something to happen to you before you are willing to make changes—like long ago when I got fired from my job. Don't wait until you get fired—quit if you know it's time to move on. Create something more for yourself. Pursue college or do whatever it is you want. Do it before someone takes away from you what you already have. You don't have to hit rock bottom to become who you are meant to be, although I must admit that needing to hit rock bottom before making a change is a belief I am continuing to overcome in my own life. We can change our lives tomorrow by being grateful for what we have today. We can change our lives today by knowing we are worth it.

## You Will Always Have More than Enough Money

One day my friend Carrie finally decided to get divorced. She was a stay-at-home-mom and had no money to her name. She was really concerned about how she would be able to leave and make it financially. She had been applying for jobs and was taking steps, but was still afraid. I whipped out a $100 bill from my wallet and asked, "May I give you $100?" She said she wouldn't take the $100, but she would take $50. I told her, "This is my gift to you. Now you have money. This is your abundance. You have $50. From this day forward, for the rest of your entire life, you will always have more than enough money."

She received that money more than three years ago, and ever since that day she's had money. She's been taken care of. She applied for her dream job as an airline flight attendant, one of 5,000 people who applied during a two-hour period. She was one of ten people who got hired. She trusted and she had faith, and for those reasons, she was taken care of.

One day, my friend Brian realized he wanted more in his life. So, he decided to write "$50,000" on a piece of paper. He slid the piece of paper into his money clip and then put it in his pocket. Every time he spent money or put money into his pocket, he looked at that piece of paper. Sure enough, thirty days later, he had his best month ever at his company and made $50,000 in one month! The cool thing about manifesting is that when you see what is possible, you allow yourself to create even more. Now his company does over five million dollars a year!

## Taking Care of Ourselves Easily and Effortlessly

During my divorce, I asked my mom for money for the first time in my life. Because her life circumstances had changed through the years, for the first time in her life she *could* help—she had the ability to be of financial support to me. And I had the courage to ask her for her help because I let my ego down. I told her how much I needed, which was about $1,500 to pay my mortgage and $600 for my car payment. I had to put my pride aside. I allowed myself to get over my stuff about money to be able to have money handed to me. My "stuff" included what I'd been taught—that nothing came easily and effortlessly, that we had to work hard, get paid for exactly what we do, and acquiring money had to be difficult. With that belief system, asking for money from someone was too easy.

I do have an amazing work ethic as a result of my upbringing, but I had to change my thoughts to know that money could come in different ways and from different places. This was a humbling piece and it was huge—to be able to allow myself to experience receiving and then know I would be better off. I was able to receive because I had given so much. When I needed it, I was able to be taken care of. I quickly got a job to get back on my feet, worked my tail off, and was able to pay her back within four weeks. The only reason I got the job and was able to get the money was because I had surrendered. I knew asking for help was the right thing for me to do in order to be able to ultimately take care of myself.

**If you let your pride win, you have you and your pride at the end of the day, which is a whole lot of nothing. But, if you let your ego down, you have a whole lot of something.**

When I got into real estate I discovered I was working ninety hours a week. I quickly realized that putting in *that* many hours wasn't what I wanted or needed, so I started to take care of myself by leaving the office each day to take a one-hour lunch break. Years before, when I had worked in retail, I'd been told that I needed to take breaks to manage the migraines I was having as a result of a car accident. At the time, however, it was impossible to take one, since in retail, I barely had time to sit and eat. As a realtor, though, because I was my own boss I could make a commitment to myself to take that break every day.

Even if you work for someone else, it's important to take time away. My mom, who has always worked hard, has eaten most of her lunches at her desk. But we are allowed time away from our desks—it's the law—so we must take it. This one simple action was a step away from that belief I had to fight—that I had to work hard for money. I realized that I had a chance to practice self-care *and* grow my business at the same time by taking lunch with people who help me in my business.

I now take even better care of myself and it shows

when it comes to money. Last year, I took three vacations and made more money than I've ever made before. It's true—taking care of ourselves is essential to receiving more in our lives. I realized early in my real estate career that I was running at half speed when I worked ninety hours in a week.

Taking a day off is important too. And, when you take a day off, you have to take it without guilt. Don't worry about the things you could have or should have done. When you give to yourself, don't feel guilty about doing so. I made the decision to take time off in my business and to do it consistently. I take one day off every week—Sundays—and on Monday I don't feel guilty. Instead, I feel refreshed.

During my divorce party, I remember my mom saying to me, "Faith, I knew you would survive." I said back to her, "That's just it, Mom. I'm done surviving...I'm thriving."

## You Don't Have to Live Out Someone Else's Life Sentence

Many people have a life sentence, like my mom who works hard for her money. That belief is true for her—that she has to work hard. Although it's her belief, it doesn't have to be mine. By watching my mom work hard her whole life, I learned to have an amazing work ethic from her, and for that I'm grateful. But I don't have to also believe that I must work myself to death for my entire life.

Your life sentence could be something completely different. The thing is, you can't live out someone else's life sentence. It's theirs, not yours. You get to choose how you live your life. Why would you choose to live out someone else's crap?

I had to reprogram my beliefs to know that things will come easily and effortlessly. When I got into real estate, people said it would be hard. They predicted that I wouldn't have a deal for six months. I kept saying back to them, "Well, that might be everyone else's sentence, but it doesn't have to be true for me." I wasn't going to buy into everyone else's belief about how the real estate business would go. I made a conscious decision not to fall victim to what everyone else believed was true. As a result, I had my first closing six weeks after I got my license.

Don't let someone else's sentence be yours. Get back to your core and ask yourself, "Do I really believe this or is this someone else's belief?" Money *can* come easily and effortlessly. Don't buy into a belief system that tells you otherwise. And...don't get stuck in the how or wait for the how to show itself before you take action. Don't be attached to the outcome either. Just ask, *How can I receive more wealth into my life*?

A friend of mine who does energy work recently got her own space for her business. She did it with faith and trusts that the clients will come. Her action tells the Universe that she's ready—she's made a leap of faith, knowing the clients will come. If you are going to take those actions and tell the Universe you are worth it and you deserve it, the Universe will deliver. It takes effort, but it doesn't need to take six months...or even five years of effort. So, take action. And remember, action can be in any form—just like my friend who needed $1,000 for her mortgage. All she had to do was say something to someone else—that was all the action that was required. Persevere through the resistance. What is on the other side is always worth it.

## Who Are You Being?

Hang around the people who are going where you are going or who are already there. If you want to be an author, hang out with authors. If you want to make $150,000 a year, hang out with people who are making $150,000 a year. Millionaires have millionaire friends. If you want to make minimum wage or take unemployment, hang out with your friends on unemployment.

I'm getting ready to hold my annual projection party and I've been asking around, "Who has a Lamborghini I can borrow? because I want a red one." You've got to make it real. You've got to be what you want, feel that it's real, and believe in it.

## Watch Scarcity Thinking

We all like a bargain, but if you go around and clip coupons for everything—you are coming from scarcity. It can be one thing to take the opportunity to enjoy a free sandwich by using a coupon every now and then, but when people get completely caught up in the free stuff, it can become a form of hoarding. It's action taken from scarcity thinking, because you use those coupons

**When you say you want to be debt-free, all the Universe hears is the word "debt."**

while thinking that one day you are not going to have enough. I truly believe that if you know you are always taken care of, you don't need a savings account—especially a savings account for a rainy day. If your money is saved for a rainy day, a rainy day will come. Hoarding money from a sense of scarcity only fuels the scarcity mentality. It's okay to have a reserve and save for something—a house or a car, for instance—but when you put money away, be clear about your reasons for doing so. Make sure your beliefs are in check. Seek to be financially free, not debt-free. Focusing on debt-free will just bring more debt.

## Don't Be Afraid to Give Money Away

When you have money, don't be afraid to give money away. If you run across someone who needs money and you have it to give, know that you will be rewarded. Just like my friend who gave the guy on the corner $100 every Friday on her way to chemo, give without attachment or expectation. Trust that you will be taken care of and you will. As with my story about giving $1 to a homeless man when I only had $2, if we know we will be taken care of, no matter what, we can afford to be generous. We will always have more than enough!

# Chapter 11: Living in Love

Living in love is a conscious decision. It's a way of being. It's how you show up in the world. When you live in love, you transform the world around you.

When my nephew was about one-and-a-half years old, he'd love on everyone and give them kisses. Then, thirty seconds later, he'd bite. That behavior didn't sit well with me. This was during the time when I had first decided to live in a constant state of love. I didn't understand his behavior, and it rubbed me the wrong way—you love me *and* hate me? He was very young, so what could I do? *I can powerfully shift how I react,* I thought. I said to myself, "I'm going to do everything out of love. When I write contracts, when I'm at the gym, when I react to him, it's all going to be out of love."

So, I practiced on him. Instead of saying, "Ow, that hurts. Don't bite me," I told him, "I like it when you hug me." I told him about the good things. I didn't focus on the bad things. Instead of "don't" or "stop," I said the opposite. When he hurt me again, I handed him to my sister and didn't say a word. The second I handed him away, he wanted me. He instantly wanted me back and wanted my love. If I had told him to stop hitting me, he would have looked at me with challenge in his eyes to hit me even more. Yet, the moment I took the love away, he made a shift. If your intention is to do everything out of love, it's amazing what results can happen. Essentially, more love. *How else can this show up in a positive way*?

When I was a kid, we went to King Soopers, our local grocery story, and saw that they were selling puppies outside the store for $1 each. My mom told my baby sister and me that we could each get one puppy. We just needed to put in half the money. Those 50 cents were the best 50 cents ever! We got CoCo and my puppy, Candy, that day.

When I was twenty-one, I still had Candy. She had been my very first dog, and I had grown up with her. At that time, she was not doing well, and we had decided we needed to put her down. The night before we were scheduled to take her to the vet, I planned it all out in my head—how the next morning was going to go and how I was going to say goodbye to her. That night, she passed away. I felt so much guilt for not being able to say goodbye that it taught me to never waste a moment with someone.

It impacted me so much that it changed how I spent

time with my grandmother in her final years. I made it a point to spend time with her and see her twice a month. I'd take her to get her hair done or do whatever I could to show her how important she was to me.

My grandmother had just won a lawsuit and received some money from it. I asked her where she wanted to go with that money. She said she had never really wanted to go anywhere. All she had ever wanted was to live long enough to raise her children—hell, she lived long enough to raise her four granddaughters and six great-grandchildren too! She had never thought that taking a trip anywhere was really possible, but we booked a trip to San Diego. And we had a great trip together. It was the best trip ever—so much so that when I dropped my grandmother back home after the trip, she gave me two kisses. This was the first time she had ever given me two kisses. She was someone who did not show affection. Even in my childhood, when I tried to kiss her, she always pulled away. So, two kisses from her was a very big deal. I will always remember that special trip for the rest of my life.

A few months later I sent her some flowers, thanking her again for the trip. The card said, "Grandma, thank you for the abundance and the trip. I love and appreciate you." She called me the morning she received them. "Faith," she said, "you are going to make me start crying at ten in the morning. The reason we had any of this is because of you. And I love and appreciate you."

Those were the last words I ever heard from my grandmother, as she passed away seven days later. I now treasure those words more than anything in my life, especially knowing that my grandmother understood how much I loved and appreciated her. And she gave me the greatest of gifts too—the chance to receive the feelings and emotion from her that she loved and appreciated me. It was a tremendous blessing to have that exchange with her as our last interaction. Imagine if those were the last words you spoke to everyone every day. I kept the card that had gone with the flowers I sent her. Because of that reminder of my simple little gesture, I was able to be at peace with her crossing over. At the same time, I saw everyone else around me full of guilt for not spending time with her or letting her know how they felt.

From then on, I committed to do everything out of love. The same week my grandmother passed, I had my annual exam and my lab results came back as abnormal with pre-cancerous cells. I didn't want to tell my family since they were still mourning her loss. I knew I couldn't put any negative energy towards myself either. With the exception of telling one girlfriend, I kept it to myself. I didn't want someone else's negative energy to affect my results.

I had to go back for a second test and asked my friend to come with me. While at the doctor's office, I thought back to what I had done during that first test. *Lay on the table...legs spread...I don't like this...it's so uncomfortable...are we done yet*? Those were the thoughts that had run through my head. I'd put negative energy into the results. The next time, seven days later, I wanted a different result and wanted to set up this exam to create a successful outcome. I knew that

I had been worried and stressed out the previous time. I reminded myself, *I'm here to get a second test out of pure love for myself. I am doing this as a loving action to myself.* What happened next? Same doctor, same table, seven days later, but...completely different results. Finding out that everything was normal reminded me how powerful our thoughts are. They can alter the results of the same exact tests.

You have to bring love to everything you do. To have love for yourself, love for your car, love for everything. When you bring love, it's amazing what the results can turn out to be.

People think hate repels, that if you hate something it will go away. But it's just the opposite. The more you hate something, the more you are going to attract it. Remember, what you think about you bring about. It's really important to make sure you keep your perspective on what you want your results to be, not on what you don't want them to be.

## Being Vulnerable and Open to Receiving Love

People don't want to get hurt. They say that a lot, "I don't want to get hurt ever" or "I don't want to get hurt again." When you are vulnerable, though, you allow yourself to receive love. People usually focus on being hurt instead of what they can receive by opening up. You set yourself up for hurt, because you are focused on the pain. Say instead, "I want to receive more love in my life." It's the same thing but stated in a positive form. It sets up all your relationships for success as well.

## Looking at Disappointments & Challenges as Gifts from the Universe

Instead of being disappointed when someone cancels an appointment, think instead, *I was just handed an hour of time*. When my MacBook fell out of my SUV, it taught me to look at the bigger gift. Momentarily, I was stuck there—devastated and beside myself that it may have just broken. Initially, I was so upset that I wasn't able to completely check myself at the door. I had to leave after dinner, because I found that I was affecting others in my family. When I got home and made that gratitude list, however, I was soon given a gift through that list and my friend Brian's response.

If you have a moment that would normally throw you off track and upset you, change it to an opportunity to do more or to do something different. That's what I attempt to do each and every time something throws me off. If someone is late or cancels, instead of being mad or angry, I say, "Look what I've been given now."

One night, I had a moment of weakness. There were some people who were "hating on me," and it really threw off my energy. I reached out and told a friend. He was there for me and reassured me that I would find and do the right thing. I considered his words and then told him that I would send them some love. "I'm going to send some of my other friends some love too as a result of this moment of weakness," I said.

I decided to send a text to six people, "You are braver than you believe and you are stronger than you know," which was also what I needed to be reminded of in that moment. The next morning, one of those friends texted me that it had been the exact words she needed to hear. As a result of my moment of weakness, I was able to help someone else. If I hadn't experienced it and reached out to someone else, I wouldn't have given her the words she needed to hear. If something negative happens, take it as an opportunity to give love rather than allow it to upset you. Instead of the *poor me, I'm late, life sucks* mentality, take it as an opportunity to give love. The cool thing is that when you need it, someone will be there for you.

Sometimes you might be mad and want to say "screw them." Instead of being pissed off or saying you want them to fuck off, send them love. Yes, it might take more effort to send them love, but it will be worth it—for both of you! That's what I did at another time when I heard from a friend that people were talking badly about me. I realized my friend was in such a negative state himself that instead of finding out from me what had taken place, he believed what was being said by others. I could have attempted to defend myself, but instead, I sent him love. I remembered to change my thoughts and shift to something more loving. So I asked my friend, "What else can I do to support you?" I knew he couldn't take my power away; I could only allow him to do so. At that point in time, he was in a very negative place in his life and on the verge of losing his home. My thought was, *Maybe this is his way of asking for help. Maybe he needs extra love right now.*

I left him a voicemail saying, "I am picturing you surrounded in abundance." Instead of acting in a negative way, I powerfully shifted the results of the situation. I acted from love rather than take it personally. As a result, he realized where my heart was—that I wanted only positive things for him and that since I wasn't attached to what others said about me, rather than add to the fire, I could put out the flame. As a result, he respected me even more.

## Living in Hope, Love and Peace

Everything happens for a reason. Sometimes, you don't know why, but there is a reason for everything.

Live in the present. By doing so, you are much more likely to see the reasons for what is happening in your life.

**I'm perfectly where I'm meant to be right now.**

Too often we live in the past or the future, not realizing that living in the present moment is the most essential way to live. Little kids are always living in the moment. Think about when you see kids playing outside or swimming in a neighborhood pool. They are not talking about going back to school on Monday. If adults are at the pool, though, what's going on in our heads? *What am I going to cook for dinner? Shoot, I forgot to make that phone call! I need to send that thank you card.* And, if we're in conversation with other friends at the pool, we're probably all rehashing what happened last week or going on about the upcoming deadlines we're facing in the week ahead. We have to remind ourselves to be present and in the moment. Enjoy the pool! The kids do.

## Finding Faith and Love

Faith is believing in something you cannot see. To manifest and create more and to be able to get what you want in life, you have to jump in with both feet. You have to move forward, at full speed, to get even more than what you thought was possible.

Whatever you believe in is true to you. That's the definition of Faith. If you believe God creates your destiny, that's true to you. If you believe you have bad luck, that's true to you. It doesn't mean it is true to everyone else, though.

One of the biggest ahas that shifted my life was the day I realized all the love I ever needed was inside of me. At the time, I was seeking all kinds of external love. I desperately wanted people to love me. I finally realized that I could love myself completely and everything else I received would be icing on the cake—I didn't need any external love to be fulfilled. In that moment, more and more blessings and love came to me, because I was giving what I needed to myself. It's like the oxygen mask on the airplane—before you put it on your kids, you need to put your mask on first. Take care of you first. Before anyone else can love you, you need to love yourself.

My friend was due to be in court for her divorce hearing. We had talked about her sending love to her ex-husband during it all because he needed it—love. When she showed up at court, she realized while she was sitting there that she needed some extra love too. So she gave it to herself as well, and it created an awareness for her. She didn't think she would need it, but she was able to give love to herself. She just kept asking herself, *What's the most loving thing I can do for myself right now? What's the loving thing I can do for him right now?*

In the past, when someone asked me, "How are you?" I told them that I was blessed. Now I add to that and tell them that I am loved. If you don't give it to yourself, why would anyone else want to give it to you? If you don't love yourself and think you are beautiful, why would anyone else?

My mission is to help people live in these two realms of love and abundance. Keep asking yourself, "What's the most loving thing I can do for myself right now?" Write a list of things you love about yourself. It can literally shift where you are going. Imagine if everyone loved themselves—what a loving, caring world we would live in!

If you aren't there yet, start with gratitude. Gratitude will help you recognize the love. Start believing in yourself. You have to believe in yourself before others will. Believe in other people and that will help you eventually believe in yourself too. Sometimes it's easier to believe in others, so start there.

# Chapter 12: Becoming Your #1 Greatest Fan

When you are your number one fan, it's a lifestyle. You say to yourself, "I'm going to do this…I know I can do that…my intentions are…" All of those statements shift things drastically. What you can achieve will be way bigger than what you even thought possible because you believe in yourself.

I remember that the coach I used to work with always stated as a lead-in to a story, "When you wake up in the morning and pass by the mirror and say, 'Oh my God! Who's that disgusting pig in the mirror?'" When I first heard him say this in front of a woman's group, I assumed

**If you are critical of yourself, you better believe everyone else will be critical of you as well.**

he was using it as an example. Instead of using it as an empowerment tool, it seemed he was using it to relate to his audience. Then, I thought, *Wait a minute! This isn't right!* It was so surprising to hear him make this statement that I couldn't hear anything else he said after that. I'm sure his intention was different, but I couldn't get past his initial statement. I began to wonder if he believed this about himself. *If you think you look like an ugly pig,* I thought, *what do you think everyone else thinks you look like*? Later, I told him he needed to be his number one fan, but right then he was being his number one critic.

We are often taught to be our biggest critic. Who knows why, but it's passed down from our parents, teachers, and peers, starting at a very young age. Even my three-year-old nephew, who plays baseball, gets pushed by his father to swing better and run faster. At that precious young age, he's already hearing criticism and a message that he's not good enough. Instead, at this young stage in his life, the message he needs to hear is, "Wow! You did a great job today! I bet you will run even faster next week. I am so proud of you." Criticism is something we are taught so early that we think it's how we are supposed to be. Then, later in life, we constantly say to ourselves that we should have worked out harder, done better, tried more, and on and on. We should have, could have, would have.

I went on to tell my coach, "When you wake up in the morning, say to yourself, 'Look at that handsome man in the mirror.'" Intrigued by this statement, he said he would start practicing. He told me that he had to actually do it while lying in bed. He would lay there and say, "I'm a very handsome man." He did it there rather than in front of the mirror so that seeing himself wouldn't prevent him from saying exactly that. As a result, he began to see himself differently. A week later when I saw him, his eyes looked much bluer, and I complimented him. He tried to deflect my compliment. Two days later, all the women at another event told him he looked handsome and asked him what he was doing. Everyone saw him differently because he began to see himself differently.

Until I brought this to attention, he hadn't realized how he was self-sabotaging himself. For him, the way he saw himself was one of the pieces he needed to fix. No one had ever called him out on what he said, most likely because people usually believe coaches hold all the answers. Yet, we have to remember that they are human too. Coaches, just like all of us, still have things to work through. Life is a journey after all, and none of us ever arrive. We are all constantly evolving.

If you are your number one fan, you'll attract more fans. If you are your number one critic, you'll attract more critics. You have to become your number one fan in all areas of your life. How you get dressed and show up first thing in the morning is going to affect how you interact the rest of the day. If you wear the wrong outfit and are uncomfortable all day long, it not only affects how you feel, but it will spread to every person who interacts with you. When people tug at their shirt all day, or cross their legs 500 times to get comfortable, their discomfort rubs off on other people. When you feel good, however, you make other people feel good too.

My intention is always to show up comfortable in

my own skin. I want other people to be comfortable in their own skin as well. However, sometimes my "comfortability" makes others uncomfortable. Sometimes, when people see things that someone else has—something they believe they don't possess—that awareness triggers a desire for them to want more for themselves. Often, they're seeing what they wish they could do for themselves. They see how they judge themselves rather than accept themselves as they are. They also see how they're not able to fully appreciate who they are. If you don't perceive yourself the way you want others to perceive you, why would anyone else?

## Honoring Yourself

Every time you have a success, give yourself a gift. I reward myself every time I have a closing on a property. There is a lot of work that goes into what I do, so I honor myself and acknowledge it by giving myself a reward. I love getting pedicures, so a simple thing I do is schedule a pedicure every single time I have a closing. I follow through with it and honor my commitment to myself. It's my reward to myself.

If you don't reward yourself, who else will? To you, a reward might be a massage or a day off. It could be anything you desire. Just commit to yourself that you will follow through with it. If you commit to yourself to go to the gym every Monday, Wednesday, and Friday, then do it. If you don't commit to yourself, who will?

Make sure the words you say to yourself are loving and caring as well. Work on yourself first before you even try to help other people. Be the best possible person you can be. Instead of saying, "I don't want this person to cheat on me," say, "I know my partner is always there for me. Without a doubt my partner is committed to me. My partner always does loving things." Remember, your wish is your command.

If something negative happens to you, honor yourself and your feelings. Many times, people don't give themselves permission to honor their feelings, a loss, or even a failure. Whatever time you need, whether it's ten minutes, ten days, or ten weeks, take care of yourself. Falling into a vicious trap of negativity or sorrow is not healthy or productive.

My broker always says to give yourself ten minutes to be mad and then get over it. If you give yourself ten minutes to be mad and you get over it, that's great. But if you are still mad, it's going to impact your next hour, the rest of your day, and possibly the rest of your week. Giving yourself permission to take the time necessary is a gentle way to allow yourself to express your emotions. If you are mad, allow yourself to be mad for ten or fifteen minutes, or for however much time you need. How fast can you get it out? If you don't honor those feelings, you might wake up the next morning and find that you're still pissed off, and you might not even remember why.

I get upset from time to time. When I do, I remind myself, "Yes, Faith, you're human. You're not a superhero. You have emotions and feelings. You have a right to be upset." I honor those feelings.

## Honor Your Commitments to Yourself

Just like rewarding yourself for your successes and following through, it's important to honor your commitments to yourself. If, for instance, you have the gym scheduled in your calendar and someone calls you to meet at that same time and you cancel the gym in order to meet with that person, then you're not honoring your own commitment. You wouldn't go to the gym during a previously scheduled meeting, so don't cancel commitments you have to yourself because other people want you do to something. Honor yourself by honoring your commitments to yourself. Believe me; in return, other people will honor you more when you do.

## Honor Your Virtue

Any time you get a chance to act in alignment with your virtue, do it. Every day, be sure your virtue is feeding your spirit and your spirit is feeding your virtue. To feed my virtue each day, I empower myself. If someone's virtue is truth, the more honest they can be with themselves, the more honest they will be able to be with others. In return, others will be honest with them.

"I don't believe it's God's mission for you to be in a church every Sunday. But I do believe it is your mission to utilize the gifts you were given in this lifetime."
- Catholic Priest

The more you believe in yourself and you're your

own cheerleader, raving yourself on, the more you will become who you are meant to be and the more you will embrace your gifts and utilize them. Know what your strengths are.

## Use Your Gifts Every Single Day

When you utilize your gifts daily, it's easy to become your number one fan. Your gifts are there to be used. The more you use them, the more opportunities you'll have to use them. Just like my gift of connection, when I was appointed chairman of the Young Professional's Network of our local realtor board, I decided to combine my current networking event with my real estate networking group. It was a leap of faith, and it ended up being a huge success. One hundred fifty people were there. Afterwards, people said it had been an amazing event! *Thank you…that's my gift…my gift is connection*. It makes perfect sense. My intention was to make it a huge success.

**Connection is my gift. You can discover your own gift. Think about what comes easy and effortlessly. Something you would do every day even without being paid to do it.**

Put yourself in situations where you can succeed by using your gifts. Opportunities will present themselves, and when an opportunity does, you will be ready.

## What's the Most Loving Thing I Can Do for Myself?

Honor your virtue by asking what's important to you. Ask yourself, "What would be a great way to validate my virtue right now? Is this honoring my virtue?" If it's not, maybe you shouldn't do it.

Since my virtue is faith, I always say, "Whatever you believe in is true to you." Virtues are your own core beliefs. The more you honor your virtues, the more they will show up and the more you will be able to utilize them to be what you are meant to be. The cool thing is, when you become your number one fan, guess what happens? You attract more fans!

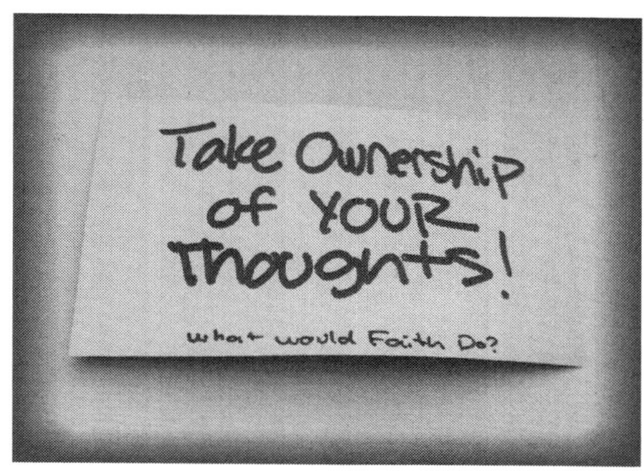


# Chapter 13: Shift Your Words and Actions and Change Your Life

Once you embrace the Universe's power, the signs show up everywhere and continuously, just like when I had my thirteen car accidents. Once I understood that the accident was a sign that my life was heading in the wrong direction, I told the Universe, "Okay, I am listening. Please send me smaller signs from now on, like tripping on the sidewalk. I promise to pay attention."

Tell the Universe you are listening to the signs you are receiving by reaffirming what you've learned and taking action on that. For example, you may get a gut feeling that you should not drive on a particular night. You listen and don't drive. The Universe will then continue to give you more signs to lead you in the right direction. Sadly, people so often have a gut feeling but don't listen and then later wish they would have paid attention.

The Universe will repeat your lessons until you learn them. Recently, a friend of mine was struggling with money—again. He was on the verge of being evicted and was several months behind on his rent. His rent was $3,500 per month, and he was clearly living beyond his means. This was the third time in the prior two years that he had gotten behind on rent and on the verge of being evicted. I decided to be bold with him. I told him, "Just so you know, the Universe will replay this same lesson until you learn it. Whatever lesson you are supposed to learn from this, learn it now, before history repeats itself."

People don't want to hear that. Instead, they would rather play the victim role. "Why me?" they ask. They'll even go so far as to say that an outside evil force is responsible for the bad things that are happening to them instead of asking what they need to learn from this so it doesn't happen again.

## Take Ownership to Learn the Lesson

Decide what the lesson is. In my friend's situation, maybe the lesson is to live within his means—not beyond them—or to not come from entitlement with the thought that *I have every right to live in a $3,500 rental property*. Maybe the lesson is to be humble and move into a $1,600 per month rental. The Universe will keep replaying the same lesson until you learn it. That's why people have the same thing show up in their lives over and over again. Take ownership and responsibility for your life instead of blaming everything that happens on everybody else.

Sometimes people will go through their entire lives without learning the lessons they were meant to learn. I've seen people in their 60s and 70s who are still not getting it. Why do you think these situations get repeated? When you hear people say, "This always happens to me," or "If I didn't have bad luck I wouldn't have any luck at all," know that those people are stuck in a vicious cycle. They are not taking ownership and responsibility for their life in order for them to shift from where they are. Those lessons will continue until they learn them.

**How to Recognize That the Universe is Trying to Tell You Something**

Are you saying:
Is this happening again?
Why does this always happen to me?

Do you notice:
Is something negative repeating in my life?

For example, if your new relationship has the same problems as your last relationship, who is the common denominator? YOU! If we haven't learned the lessons in a past relationship, those opportunities to learn will continue to show up in the next one. For instance, if you have issues with trust because you were cheated on in a past relationship, until you clear up those trust issues, they will show up again and again.

### Seek Guidance

To learn the lesson, ask a question or seek guidance. Listen and see what comes back. It isn't as though the Universe sends you a message in a cloud for you to receive. It's in the little ways that you will usually get your answers. The answer may come that day, the next day, or even many days later. Here's a good statement to proclaim to the Universe: "Let me have more clarity on the next step I'm supposed to take." When you seek assistance from the Universe, you can receive your answers from anywhere. It may be in the form of a yellow signal light. Maybe the answer you need is to slow down, so pay attention.

**About Money**
**I have a friend who I loaned a large amount of money to and they still haven't paid me back a year later. I told them, "I highly recommend you pay me back, because until you do, the Universe will continue to take away from you and bless me. I have already done my good deed."**

Meditation is a great way to listen for the answers. Spend time each week in meditation—whatever form speaks to you. I use a blended form of guided meditation that I do twice a week for two hours each time. It's too hard for me to sit in a room and just be quiet, so I need a guided process to allow me to tap into those answers from the Universe. Meditation can help you receive more clarity and "create space for something new."

## Credentials

Once you have moved through the pain and are on the other side, then it becomes your credential. For example, if you are going through a divorce that is painful, you probably won't be able to help others while you are still going through yours. Once you are divorced, however, and have survived the experience, then it becomes your credential. Then, you have the tools to help others do the same. Each time you learn a lesson, you get more credentials. They help you move from being in the lesson to helping others with that same lesson. You can't help other people until you've gone through something yourself. Once you have gone through it, you can help and teach other people—then you can learn more on a whole different level.

## Things Faith Would Never Say

- That sucks…
- I wish…
- I should have…
- I could have…
- I would have…
- I hate that…
- You made me…
- I don't have…
- I hope…
- I'm lucky…
- Good luck…
- I can't….
- I know…
- My biggest fear is…

Since thoughts are extremely powerful in creating your life, the words and language you use are critical to creating exactly what you do want instead of what you don't want. Here are a few examples of how not to use the words listed above:

If a friend tells you they have an event, a show, or some other project, don't chime in with the words we often hear—"Good luck!" Instead, say something like, "I wish you the best," or "Have fun tonight." It's not luck that you are offering—it's good wishes, even blessings. Try to use words that can really help them.

"That sucks" is one of the worst things you can say to someone. You actually feed the fire as soon as you say that phrase, because those words justify or solidify someone's pain or anger. People think they are relating to someone else, that they are empathizing by using such a phrase, but you can empathize without using the words "that sucks." Even by saying something like, "I hear you," or "I hate it when that happens," adds more negative energy to their situation. Instead, use the phrase that we've talked about before—"at least." By saying something like, "*At least* you are okay. What could you do differently next time?" you are offering them the opportunity to move forward and shift their energy.

"I hate" is another powerful phrase that creates more negativity around you and the situation. "I should, could, or would have..." Don't get caught up in these words either. Put them into a positive form and take ownership of your actions.

An important realization with language is to notice how you discount the decisions you make—good or bad. Everything is divinely inspired, so don't take away from what happened because something else didn't turn out exactly as you expected. Just the other day, I walked out of the office and when I got to my car, I realized my keys were still at my desk. *I guess I was meant to be delayed,* I thought. I arrived five minutes later than I wanted, but that's what was meant to happen. What if I missed a car accident by being five minutes later than I'd anticipated?

It's the things we don't see and don't realize that can impact us. If you had a window of opportunity where you could see what might have happened, you would probably think differently and realize how much the divine is at work in your life, but we don't always get to see that. It's great when we do, so look for it. At the very least, trust that there is a bigger picture at work.

We talked about "my biggest fear..." previously and about how important it is to be mindful of proclaiming your biggest fear out loud or even focusing on your fears internally. Fear is huge. People attract their biggest fear to themselves, because what you think about you bring about. In my life, being alone was my biggest fear. When my husband walked out on me, I thought *Wow! Is that what I created*? I do believe our thoughts are *that* powerful. When I was going through my divorce, I wrote in my journal every night, "OMG, I am so lonely." So, the Universe said, "You want to be lonely? Poof! Your wish is your command." As I talked about in a previous chapter, when I was so focused on being alone, my dog Buddy passed away. Remember, what you think about you bring about, so focus on what you do want.

"I know." When people tell me they know, I ask them,

"Why am I even telling you then if you already know?" When you say "I know," you are shutting off the Universe. I was training a gal one time on a unique system in our company. After each step I showed her, she said, "I know." About an hour or so into listening to her say that, I asked, "How would you know that? Do you need me to train you or not? If you think you know everything, why am I wasting my time?" It's not that people know. It's a conditioned response, and it blocks you from receiving more.

That conditioned response is often a conscious way to not receive more. People say it because they're not really ready to hear or receive more. Sometimes, they have the knowledge already but they aren't using it. Their "I know" is a way to block more reminders of what they already know. Sometimes, they don't know how to implement what they do know. Again, they don't want to face that knowledge. To help someone when they respond with "I know," you can say, "OK, how can I help you now?" or "What is it that you need right now? How can I be of service and support to you?" That might just help them let go of their need to resist.

## Things Faith Would Never DO

Don't feel guilty for the actions you take.

Something as simple as taking a nap, or sleeping in, or as big as going away on vacation for a few days—often, people will look back and feel guilty for doing them. *Oh, I should've gotten up. Why did I allow myself to sleep so late*? If you are going to allow yourself to sleep in or take a nap, do not put guilt on yourself immediately afterwards. If you do feel guilty, essentially you erase that hour you took for that nap. You take it and all its benefits away from you. Don't feel guilty for a vacation, a nap, or anything you've done. Don't beat yourself up for yesterday, just learn from it.

You can't go back and change the past.

I don't regret what I've done, but I do focus on how I can do better in the future. Thinking about the future is a way to shift it to the positive. You might be thinking, *Wow, I can't believe I was dating that guy a year-and-a-half ago.* Allow yourself to not feel guilty because that's all you knew at the time. People do the very best they can in the moment.

My mom beat my dad with roses long ago, but she would never do that today. It was the best she could do at that time. As soon as you can embrace that concept—that we are all doing the best we can with the tools we have—you will learn your lessons faster. Instead of feeling shame for what went wrong ask, "How can I do better next time?" Although it may be hard to give yourself credit—that yes, you did the very best you could at that moment in time—making that shift in perspective will allow you to move forward. It may be easier to offer that perspective to others, but remember; if you are going to give others that same credit you might as well give it to yourself first.

Don't ever wish harm upon others.

If you do, that harm will come back to you. Whatever you put out into the Universe comes back to you tenfold.

When I was fifteen, I was walking down the street and two teenagers came around a corner way too fast and practically hit me. My immediate response was, "You stupid bitch, I hope you get in an accident." I was driving down the road with my friends a couple of hours later, and sure enough, she got into an accident. I've had thirteen accidents in my life, so how is that for coming back tenfold?

Don't wish harm upon anyone. If people would change this one thing and take ownership of their thoughts, that one change would powerfully impact the world. Send people love instead. I could have simply said, "I wish she would slow down," or "Man, she could use some extra love right now." Imagine how different the results in my own life might have been if I had focused on love instead.

When I send people love, even the road-rage people on the street, it makes people check themselves at the door. It makes people stop and think. I blow kisses to people who are angry—so people will check themselves. They just need love.

Be aware of your words and actions so they don't sabotage you.

You can see how confident or cocky someone is, or how low someone's self-esteem might be, by giving them a compliment and then observing their response. First, find something genuine to compliment someone about. If they look down and say, "Oh, I got this on sale," it reflects that they are most likely insecure and don't receive compliments well. That also means they don't receive other things well either. They need to work on receiving in general. Don't tell people where you got something or how much you paid for it when you are offered a compliment. Unless they ask how much it was or where you got it, just simply say thank you.

If you give someone a compliment and they say, "Yeah, I know," then they are probably cocky. My thought is, *Why would I want to compliment them again*?

Then there are those people who simply say, "Thank you." That's all you really need to say. Not, "Oh, this old thing," or "I got it on clearance at Wal-Mart." When people aren't used to receiving, they downsize the compliments coming their way. Even "I know" is a good way to block receiving. It doesn't mean they are confident, however, just cocky. They are over-compensating for something else in their life.

When you are able to say a simple thank you, it's a great way to tell the Universe you are ready to receive. Literally, look someone in the eye when they compliment you and say "Thank you." If they ask where you got your dress or your shirt, then tell them, but don't tell them about the sale or the thrift store where you got it if they didn't ask. The more compliments you are able to receive, the more compliments you'll get.

When you leave your house knowing you look and feel good, you will get a bunch of compliments. It's because of how you feel about yourself—people feel your goodness. There's another thing you can do to really take in and solidify for yourself the compliments you receive from others. If someone says, "You look so beautiful." Say, "Thank you, I feel beautiful." They win because you were truly listening and they just helped you feel good, and you win because you just took ownership of it. When you repeat their words, it makes them feel good as well. Receiving a compliment helps you shift your own energy into gratitude. And that attracts even more good into your life. Likewise, you can immediately shift someone else's energy when you compliment them.

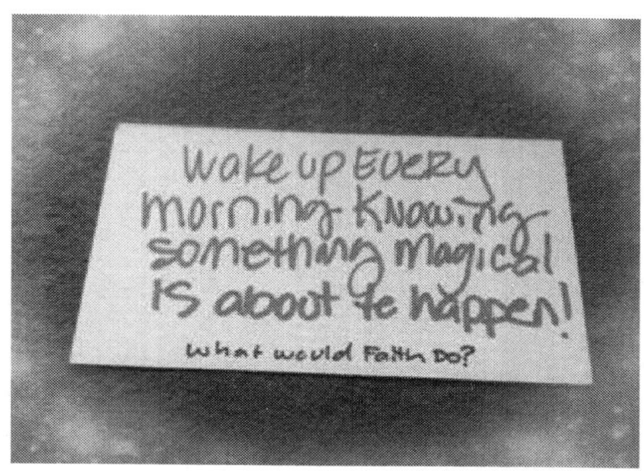


# Chapter 14: Power of Intention

The power of intention pleasantly surprises me on a daily basis. I believe it's important to state your intentions every day. Write them down, tell an accountability partner, put it in a F.U.E.L. book—do whatever you need to do to clearly state your intentions.

The majority of the world wakes up every day and stumbles through their day. Things just happen to and around them. What if you had an opportunity to choose what happened for you during the day each and every day?

I love to tell myself, "Wake up every morning knowing something magical is about to happen." That is an intention, almost like an affirmation, but even more powerful. Creating the intention for what you want to happen is like playing a game with the Universe. When you state or write down an intention and it comes true that same day, it reminds you how powerful your thoughts are and that you can create even more. At four in the afternoon, when I get an email saying the short sale was approved, after having written it down that morning, I think *Wow, I created that! I had been working on it for four months, but the day we wrote it down, it happened.*

Intentions help you play bigger. They will help you create and intend more every day. Once the little things happen, you still start to say, "Huh, what can I create today?" It allows you to create what you want instead of the Universe randomly handing you things throughout the day. When you make your intentions, you can be as vague or as a specific as you want. I might say, for instance, that I want to get 123 Elm Street under contract today. That's a very specific request. Or my intention may be to pick up a new client today. That client could come from anywhere. People set goals all the time, but the words "I intend" or "my intention is" are much more powerful than "my goal is." Intention is movement and action to make it happen.

The most important thing after stating your intention is to take some kind of action to make that intention happen. If your intention is to pick up a new client, you might post something about your business on Facebook, or call a girlfriend and ask her to lunch, or do something else to follow up with your intention. You can't simply write "to get a million dollars today," and then lay on the couch for the rest of the day. You have to follow through with your intentions.

To take this concept one step further, it's important to make sure your intentions are things you really want. If you think to yourself, *Yeah...that might be nice*, your statement is not really from the heart. In fact, it's not either a statement or declaration. It's kind of wishy-washy. So, to get to your true intentions, you might start by asking yourself, *What is it I am really seeking*? *Why do I want that*? Be sure that your intentions line up with how you feel about those things that you desire.

## Daily & Hourly Intentions

Every morning I look at my appointments and I'll say, "Okay, I have a call at 10:00 a.m., so my intention is to have an amazing call today when I speak to that person. I have lunch at 12:00 p.m., so my intention is to show up exactly how my friend needs me to show up today." I break it down hourly into what I want to create. The intention can shift throughout the day depending on what comes up. Perhaps I have some extra time or something changes in my plans for the day. It's amazing how being on time or picking the right place for dinner can be intentional. People think things usually happen by accident, but if you have a chance to set something up intentionally, the results can be powerful. Oh, and by the way, I don't believe anything happens by accident or coincidence.

I was at a three-day weekend workshop where my intention was to show up exactly how everyone else in the room needed me to show up, to be the tool or the portal for them. By the end of the three days, people came up to me saying how my story and my being there had impacted their lives. Thank God I made that intention. About five weeks later, a girlfriend who I had met at that weekend workshop told me the best gift she had received from that weekend was me. "You were my gift," she said. Imagine if I hadn't said those words, "I'm going to show up exactly how everyone else needs me today." I wouldn't have made the most amazing friendship that I have now.

Writing your intentions down and sharing them with an accountability partner, like I do with my women's group or my assistant, is powerful. It's that collective thought that I've talked about before. If you want to intend or create something, share it with a group who can help you hold that intention. Then you'll have ten or fifteen other women who want the same thing for you. For example, at my mastermind group, we regularly share our intentions. My friend Alex told us that she was ready to receive her soulmate. We were all in agreement and supportive of her intention. The cool thing is that she met him on Match.com a couple months later, in January 2012. She then moved in with him in March and was married in October 2012. How powerful is that?

## Expectations Versus Intentions

There is a difference between an expectation and an intention. Let's say you are going on a date tonight and you say, "My intention is to have an amazing time tonight." It's pretty vague, so that intention could mean anything—your plans are to go out for dinner, a movie, and a glass of wine afterwards. Your intention is to have an amazing time in the midst of the things you're planning to do. But if you are thinking, "He better pay for everything!" that's an expectation. If you say you are going to have an amazing time, it could include your date paying for everything, but you are not setting it up as an expectation. Having your date pay for everything would be icing on the cake.

People sabotage themselves by having expectations of other people. People think others should or should not show up in a certain way. Your expectations can hinder them from showing up in the best light possible. So don't expect, intend.

Expectations come from entitlement. It's the belief that other people have to do something that you want them to do. Intention is about awareness and consciousness. Expectations are something that you believe or think you should have—something you believe you are entitled to. Intentions are something that you ask for, take action on, and intend to receive each and every day.

Intentions are about how *you* are showing up, and expectations are about how *other people* are showing up. Expectations are external, whereas intentions are internal. Intentions take ownership. Expectations put someone else in charge of your happiness, well-being, and success. You put your fate in someone else's hands when you create expectations, yet the power is in your hands when you create intentions.

## Creating a Sense of Daily Urgency

We hear it all the time. In a month from now I'll do this, or two years from now I'll buy a house, start a business, take that trip. Well, what if you can start shifting things today? What if you start preparing today?

A girlfriend of mine told her mom that she was tired of her mom renting and that she should talk to me about buying a house. Her mom didn't believe it was possible and hadn't even looked into what it would take to buy a house, but she believed in her daughter enough that she was at least willing to talk to me and see how I could help. I spoke with her mom, had her talk to my lender, and within two weeks we were in the car looking at properties. When we closed on a house a short time later, her mom said, "You know what Faith, who would have thought that someone who made $12 an hour could own a house?"

We created a sense of urgency about something that she hadn't believed was a possibility for her. Helping her buy a house became a huge gift. All she needed to do was give it an ounce of energy and intention, see the possibility of it, have faith, and allow it to happen. As a result, she has now realized that she is capable of more and is even seeking a better job. She also now socializes and has people over to her house. Not only does she see the possibility of more in her own life, but she encourages others to seek more as well. She is now the example to her family and friends by having a home of her own and seeking a new job and better relationships for herself.

Focus on what you can do today. Start doing that. If

your intention is to go to Hawaii next Christmas, cut out pictures of Hawaii and put it on your vision board. Google hotels and find out how much money you'll need to get there. Those are things you can do immediately to turn those intentions into realities for the future.

One more thing...be sure to add the words "or more" to everything you intend. My intention is to pick up five *or more* new clients by the next meeting. My intention is to have a million dollar *or more* listing. I hear people say that their intention is to make $40,000 for the year. What if you could do that by June? Don't limit yourself by time. What if you could do it in six weeks or six months? Take the limitations out of your intentions. Always add the *more* so you don't ever limit yourself.

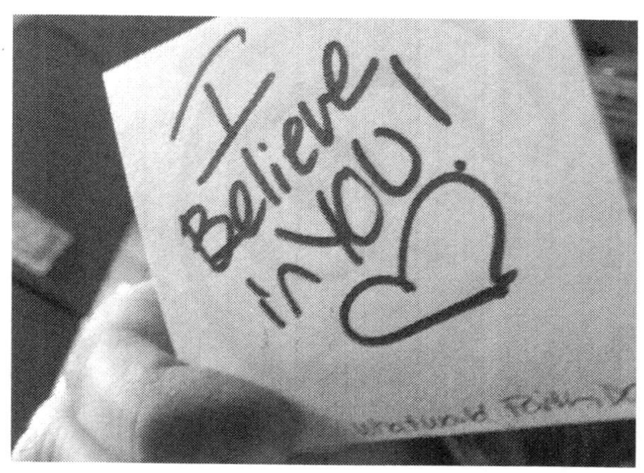


# Chapter 15: Manifesting Greatness

What if you could manifest what you want in life? What if you could create your destiny and manifest greatness? It's possible, and in my life I see miracles happen all the time, but they happen because I believe.

As I was writing this book, I witnessed another miracle with my friend Maricela, who had cured herself of cancer through the power of love. She asked me to go with her to her second MRI to make sure her cancer hadn't come back. For weeks, we had been preparing for it. I was constantly sending her love and picturing her cancer free. We believed she had been freed from it. On the day the results of her MRI came back, we found out she was indeed cancer free. She walked out of the doctor's office and into the waiting room where I was sitting.

With her arms up in the air, she exclaimed, "I am cancer FREE!" It had all happened without chemotherapy and radiation. She beat and conquered her cancer with the power of love.

The first thing you have to do is take ownership of your thoughts and realize your thoughts do create things. Think about it. You are driving down the road and you think, *I haven't had a flat tire in a long time*. Five days later…bump, bump, bump. *What just happened*? Your energy was enough to create that. Then, instead of taking ownership for creating this situation, you blame the idiot who left nails out on the road. But if you back track your thoughts, you'll see it was really your responsibility.

The key to manifesting is that you have to take ownership of both—the positive and the negative. And remember, you only need 51% of your thoughts to be positive. It isn't that you can't think those negative things, but as soon as you recognize you are thinking negative thoughts, it's important to shift your thinking. *What can I do differently*? *What thoughts can I shift now to shift my future*?

When people begin to take ownership, often, they also begin to take on a lot of blame or shame. *Oh, I created this abuse*? *I created all this negativity*? We don't need to feel blame, shame, or guilt. Those three things bring more negativity into our lives and they are self-sabotaging. When you feel these negative emotions, you are in the same energetically negative realm as you were when the negative incident or situation occurred. When we're in a victim state, we want to blame others, including ourselves. Yet, forgiveness is essential. We all do the best we can at the time with the knowledge we have. When we allow ourselves to see what we can learn from a situation or experience and acknowledge that everyone does the very best they can, that's when the growth comes in. Take ownership so you can create more positive thoughts. Manifesting all comes down to what you are thinking about.

A few years ago, I really wanted to attend a three-day workshop by Greg Mooers. For some reason, it just didn't seem to be manifesting for me. I had put a deposit down on the $2,500 event about a year earlier and kept waiting for the money to show up. Then, the Monday before the weekend event, my friend called me and asked, "Faith, did you want to go to 'Authen Talk?'" *Uh, yeah!* "Well, I just got a call from them," she said, "and they offered me a gift where I can bring a friend for free." I immediately rearranged my schedule and made it happen. Four days later, I was there.

At one point during the weekend, we did an exercise where we needed to get as many votes for ourselves as possible without speaking. We weren't allowed to talk at all, but we could pretty much do anything else. The person with the most votes would win the next level of the workshop series, "LiFormula." I had already written in my journal during that weekend that I was going to attend "LiFormula" for free, before I even knew it was possible. As soon as he told us about the opportunity to win, I said to myself, "I'm going to win that!"

We started the exercise and it was a good three or four minutes before anyone could even figure out what to do. I was thinking about what my strategy could be and kept telling myself, "Faith, you have the power to create this." My beautiful friend, Courtney, who I had met there and am still friends with today, was holding up three fingers. At first, I thought she meant that she had three votes, but then I realized she wanted the third prize. The first prize was the "LiFormula" weekend, second prize was individual coaching, and third was online training. Then, my friend Nancy, who'd invited me, and had already done "LiFormula," indicated she wanted the second place prize. *Now, I know how I can make this happen*. They knew what they wanted as well, so the energy was there. I wanted to hand deliver those gifts to them. I literally started to line people up like dominoes behind the two of them. People were catching on and someone quickly wrote down prize #1, prize #2, and prize #3 on a piece of paper.

It was so intense that immediately some people jumped out of the game. A lady who jumped ship started to talk, because no one said she couldn't. "Oh my gosh," she said, "I see what Faith is doing. Faith wants the number one prize, Nancy wants the number two prize, and Courtney wants the third place prize. So, make sure that more of you line up behind Faith, then Nancy, then Courtney," she instructed. I had fifteen people behind me, Nancy had eight, and Courtney had three. After about five minutes of standing there in anticipation, Greg Mooers asked, "Are you guys done?" We all nodded our heads YES! YES! since we still couldn't talk. "Congratulations!" he said and then confirmed that Courtney, Nancy, and I had each won the prizes we wanted.

He then told us that we had done the exercise in

record time; that he had done the exercise 100 times before, and just the weekend before it had taken five-and-a-half hours for the group to find a solution. He was shocked. "You guys did this exercise in seventeen minutes. I've never seen it happen this quickly. Who would have thought that someone named Faith, whose virtue is *faith*, would win this? It makes perfect sense, though, doesn't it?" What I learned right then is that if you truly believe in manifesting and declare to the Universe what you want, it rearranges everything in the Universe to make it happen, just like pawns on a chessboard. It was one of the most powerful examples of manifesting I had ever seen, witnessed, and created. I won a $2,500 three-day weekend out of a free weekend that I'd already manifested.

## How to Manifest

As *The Secret* says, if you want something now, you've got to feel as if you've already received it. Feeling is critical to turning it into reality. That's the reason I have my projection parties. These parties were inspired by the concept of collective thought. The party is a "vision board in action." Everyone in attendance comes as if they have already achieved whatever it is they want to achieve for the year. They act out their visions—projecting it on to everyone else who is there. And all who see what their vision looks like now have that imagery in their own hearts and minds too. For instance, two years ago, I came to the projection party dressed like a princess with my Cinderella shoes on. I told the friends in attendance how I had met my Prince Charming and that he was tall, dark, and handsome.

Adriana, in full belief, exclaimed, "Oh my gosh, Faith, what is his name?"

In that moment, she made it that much more real for me. I had said it with such belief and conviction that she believed it was already true, even though we were at the projection party. At that same party, another friend came as if she were pregnant. The party was in January, and sure enough, Jessica not only got pregnant but delivered that baby within the same year. It's the feeling behind it that makes it manifest. At those parties, we feel *it* and act as if *it* is already real. It's an exciting, high-vibrating night of joy and fun.

In 2012, the server at the restaurant where we held our party said to me, "Thank you to all of you for your positive energy. We don't see that very often." She also thought that everything that had happened that night was real, including me having my own TV show on the Oprah channel.

And at the beginning of this year, Adriana came to the projection party wearing an engagement ring from her partner. I reacted and thought it was real. I cannot wait for that dream to powerfully manifest for her this year.

There are so many ways to make *manifesting* real for you. Here are the things that work for me: focused energy, feeling it, sharing that vision with other people, writing it down, creating a vision board. These are all things you can do to create what you want.

Vision boards are one of my favorite things to do.

They are intensely powerful. The vision board I created in 2010 had a picture of my ex-boyfriend with his roommate's Chihuahua. I wanted a Chihuahua, so I used that picture of him with the dog on his lap for my vision board. I wanted to manifest the perfect Chihuahua, and five days after creating that vision board, she was born on January 7th. Four weeks later, on February 7th, she was in my hands. Then, all of a sudden, on March 7th, my ex-boyfriend came back into my life too. That's when I realized that he was on the vision board with the Chihuahua. I reminded myself, *Be careful what you wish for.* Since I had only wanted to manifest my perfect dog, I needed to change my board and remove the picture of him. The photo of both the Chihuahua and my ex-boyfriend had been so powerful that I had attracted both into my life!

When creating a vision board, something important to remember is that if you are in a relationship and want to stay in that relationship, you need to include your partner in your vision. It's amazing how many times I see my friends not include their partners on their vision board and then find themselves separated or dealing with marital problems. *Well, what was your vision, what was your focus*? As a couple, make sure you put each other on your vision boards.

It's also important to recognize afterwards what you did manifest. My beautiful friend, Andrea Costantine, gave me a manifesting jar. It's an empty jar that you fill up with little slips of paper. You write down on each piece of paper what you have ALREADY manifested into your life through the power of intention. Then, you add it to your jar and watch it fill up. I love my jar! It has things like my trip to the Broadmoor and free Avalanche hockey tickets in there. And if there is ever a day when I'm feeling down, I open my jar and reflect on all the good things I have already attracted into my life.

## Managing Doubt

To manage doubt, you have to believe, and belief is one of the steps to manifesting. You can ask for what you want all day long, but if you don't believe it's possible, or in your realm of possibility, you are wasting your breath. You have to ask yourself, "Am I honestly capable of receiving this?" If not, just start working towards it. Start shifting those beliefs to what's possible.

Take Donald Trump for example. Here's a man who has lost it all and gained it back again, because he believed it was possible. He has the same twenty-four hours that we do. He wasn't handed anything different than we are handed, but somewhere deep inside he has believed it was possible. Donald Trump was five million dollars in debt when he asked to borrow five million more. He knew he could make it all again. He believed in himself. Now he's a billionaire.

**Four Steps to Manifesting**

**1. Ask**
**2. Believe**
**3. Take action**
**4. Don't worry about the how**

You have to manage your beliefs and your doubts. Many people wait until they hit rock bottom to become who they are meant to be. But that's just a hidden belief that you need to hit rock bottom to manifest your greatness. What if you didn't have to hit rock bottom before you became who you were meant to be? You have to eliminate the beliefs you don't even know you have—all those beliefs that hold you back, including the beliefs you have about yourself. Those beliefs are what can hold you back and that's why my ultimate goal is to have seven billion people know I believe in them—so I can pass along an ounce of faith to every human being. That's all someone needs is to know someone else believes in them. *If she believes in me, why shouldn't I*?

Managing doubt takes effort. If you doubt something for one second, it alters the outcome. During the last presidential election, I knew without a doubt that the president was going to be reelected. I knew it without a doubt. I didn't doubt it for one second. You have to believe that something is possible to create it. The president had to believe he would get re-elected as well. You have to believe with complete conviction and not doubt it for a second, no matter what.

If you don't love yourself and think you are beautiful, why would anyone else? The same is true with belief. If you don't believe it's possible, why would anyone else? Just notice where your belief is and see how you can start believing in yourself more.

When you have doubt, you have to instantly turn it around. Stop those thoughts that tell you things like, "Don't push yourself to be a top producer. That's scary, and that's not in your realm." That's your ego talking. Your ego has its place to protect you, so say to it, "Thank you for showing up, but I'm still going to believe anyway. I still know it's possible."

Take ownership of your own emotions about things

and recognize them for what they are. *Why is my ego showing up? Why do I have doubt about this? What can I shift right now?* When you have doubt it creates a spiral of negativity. *What was I thinking? Why did I do that? I did a horrible job today, and I probably did a horrible job yesterday. I probably shouldn't be doing this at all.* The negative spiral happens fast; it travels ten times faster than positive energy. It can shift things in one second. As soon as you have doubt, immediately check it at the door.

## Find the Story Inside You

To stop the doubt, find the story inside you. Every single time I have doubt I stop myself in my tracks and say, "Faith, if I can help my friend Maricela cure herself of cancer, I can do anything." Everyone has a story within themselves. If I have doubt, I remind myself of that story. What happens when you tell your story, or even hear mine? It makes you believe.

I was telling a friend about my doubt story and asked her about the story in her life. She proceeded to tell me about her son going to college. She knew he would, but everyone else doubted it. People told her, "You don't have any money saved. You are a single mom. How are you going to do it?" He got a full scholarship and all she had to pay was $150. She said she knew right then and there that she had never doubted it for one second. She manifested this amazing gift. That's her doubt moment. If she

**What's the story inside you?**

ever has doubt at any point during the rest of her life, all she has to do is go to that feeling she had when he received that scholarship and remember how much joy and gratitude and appreciation she had for herself for believing that it was possible. It's just another reminder how powerful belief is. Everyone else may doubt you, but if you believe, that is all that matters.

## It's Bigger than You Could Even Imagine

If someone had told me five years ago that I would write a book, I would have said, "Yeah, right." But a year-and-a-half ago, I started to say, "It's bigger than I could imagine." Everything is. Just eating lunch is bigger than I could imagine. When you believe bigger than what you've been taught, a big giant shift will happen. When those things happen, then you start to ask, "What else is possible?" You have to give yourself permission to believe in something different.

Bigger than you could imagine is also living beyond your imagination. The more you help yourself, the more you can help others. The more money you have, the more gifts you can create, and the more you have to give. It's not a selfish act at all, but one of the most loving acts you can do for yourself—believing you deserve as much as anyone else.

Make such a powerful shift in yourself that it causes other people to shift too. We cannot change anyone, and that is not our purpose on this earth. It is not our job to change other people. We can only focus on ourselves. When you make such a powerful shift in yourself, though, it causes other people to shift—it invites them to do the same.

A great example is the story I told before about judgment and how it helped my own sister. When I made a powerful shift about not allowing judgment to bother me anymore, she shifted on her own and released her own judgment. If I had known that was going to be the result, I would have shifted a long time ago. The same is true with my coach who thought he looked like an ugly pig. Once he shifted his thoughts, people saw him differently. He made such a powerful shift in himself that we physically saw him differently.

Think about the energy of people who have slumped shoulders, those who don't make eye contact or hide behind someone else. These are all things people do because they don't want to be noticed. Yet, the men or women who walk into a room looking and feeling confident make you think, *Who was that*? *Who just walked in*? We have that response because the energy in that person says, "It is right for me to be here. I am bringing something to the table." The people in the room can sense their energy when they walk in—they know these men and women are important and sense that they bring value. They radiate, and others can feel it.

## Writing Your Personal Story Based on What You Want, Not What History Has Given You

People think they are destined to be overweight, destined to have heart disease, destined to die at a young age, or destined to be poor. My physical body is a great example. During my entire life, my mom has been overweight. I've never known her to look any different. When I was a teenager I used to starve myself. I did 500 sit-ups a day. I weighed 135 pounds. I thought I was heavy at that time. When I look at those pictures, I see that I was thinner than my eighteen-year-old niece is right now. But I thought I was overweight. And I believed it was genetic. *My mom was heavy, so I am destined to be heavy too.* I told my niece last Christmas that the reason why my sisters and I are all heavy is because we fell into that trap of believing we were destined to be heavy. "You are at a perfect weight right now," I told her. "Don't fall into the belief I fell into about it. It's a trap."

People have those kinds of beliefs about money, about success, and about working hard, to name a few. I had that "working hard" belief as well—I had to change that thought process. *Everyone else might have to work hard, but I don't have to.* I said this to myself over and over again. Otherwise, I would have ended up working three jobs like my mom did for seven years—McDonalds from 6:00 to 9:00 a.m. Monday through Friday, then an insurance job from 9:00 a.m.to 6:00 p.m. Monday through Friday, then every Saturday and Sunday at Wal-Mart. Three jobs! Seven days a week!

Growing up I thought that was what a person had to do—work your ass off because nothing is ever handed to you. It was a powerful shift when I realized that my belief was my mom's sentence, but it didn't have to be mine. Maybe those beliefs were passed on to her, but I didn't have to believe in them—just like the physical inheritance of diabetes or heart disease or some other medical or physical condition. Usually when someone says it's hereditary, we believe it. Yet that belief, that something is hereditary, is one of the most debilitating thoughts.

**Exercise**

**Write all the beliefs you have about life, success, money. Ask, "Are these beliefs serving me?" If not, put them into a positive form and make them into an affirmation.**

Use the tools we've mentioned before. *Is it my belief or my mom's belief? Does that belong to me or society?* Is that my shit or theirs? Send it back. Neutralize it. It's never too late to change it—whatever the belief is that no longer serves you. Say to yourself, "My intention is to release any hidden belief that no longer serves me. I may not even know what that means, but whatever is no longer serving me, I release it." Sometimes we have beliefs that serve a purpose. For instance, my mom's belief was a survival mechanism. She worked hard, and as a result, kept a roof over our heads. But we don't always need those beliefs later on in life. We can release them and say that they no longer serve us.

## The Possibility of Full Belief

I went to an event recently and said, "Oh, I'm going to win the door prize." People looked at me like I was crazy. Then, I did win the door prize and I got another call the next morning about another prize I had won for a free facial. Those things happen all the time, yet it's mathematically impossible to make sense of how often I win. They happen because I truly believe they're possible. When you walk into a place and state that you are going to win the door prize, and then you do, people automatically believe in you. It's pretty cool.

Work your way up to a higher confidence level when it comes to manifesting. Start with free lunch. "I'm going to receive free lunch today." Once you get free lunch, your brain says, "Okay, this worked." Then you go bigger and bigger and bigger.

My intention is to manifest $200,000. I've manifested free vacations, weekends away, Rockies games, so I know this is possible too. Start little with something that's easy and something that you are going to succeed at. It's like a game you can play with the Universe. *What else is possible? If I can manifest free lunch, what about free dinner? What about that trip? What about that iPad?* The most important thing is not to worry about the how. If you are going to manifest a free trip, is that going to come from your boss? Probably not. But what if your best friend just inherited a bunch of money and wants to take you on a trip? People usually want to see how they are going to get something. Don't worry about the how; just believe it's possible.

It's the same with money. Money doesn't have to come only from your job; it can come from anywhere. Whenever I receive checks in the mail, they're not from my real estate business. They're because I am manifesting money from somewhere else. Every time I go to the mailbox, I repeat, "There are checks in the mail, checks in the mail." I believe this so much that when I was housesitting for my sister, I went to check her mailbox and I found myself saying it for her, "Checks in the mail, checks in the mail." I laughed at myself. *Faith! You believe in this so much, you're manifesting and this isn't even my mailbox. It's so engrained in me that now it's not even conscious.* Later, I asked my sister if she had received any checks in the mail—she had. She'd received a $50 rebate check in the mail. The how is the biggest step that people have to overcome to embrace manifesting.

Remember, believe first. Don't worry about the how. Manifest. Keep asking what else is possible?

## Personal Purpose Statement

My personal statement is, "Each and every day my intention is to empower every single person I interact with and leave a positive impression on every person to create more love and abundance, to lead by example and live authentically, so other people can do the same for themselves—to show up so powerfully that other people can do the same."

A purpose statement is both personal and intentional. It's something you want to "be" every single day in your life. It's your purpose, so put it into a statement that you can remember and live. Once you realize your purpose and start being intentional about it, it's amazing how situations and circumstances show up every single day so you can fulfill your purpose. You get to fulfill those opportunities all the time.

To create your purpose statement, look at your gifts,

virtues, and core beliefs. It will allow you to purposefully live your life, instead of living it by accident or coincidence. It's all about intention. Rather than stumble through your days, you can wake up and intentionally live your day. Instead of living in a reactive state, you are deliberate.

Having your purpose statement lets you know that "at least" you currently want to live in that purpose. That purpose, however, may shift, which means your purpose statement needs to shift. Your purpose statement is bigger than today, so you don't have to be attached to your purpose statement. Let it be your guide. It may shift so move with it. Even as things change, having a purpose statement is about continuing to live intentionally. Whether your purpose statement needs to change every six months or every six years, it doesn't matter. Because no matter when things shift, "at least" you'll know you were living your purpose during that time. You are creating your life in a meaningful way.

## Living in the Past, Present, Future

Goal-oriented people live in the future. People who are victims or are fear-based live in the past. When you live in the present, you are neither in fear or expectation. You are truly grateful and present for what you have now.

When I got my puppy, it was a prime example of how to live in the present. You never say to a puppy, "Oh, I can't wait for you to grow up." No, if anything, you want to bottle their puppy breath. You don't want that moment to go away. Living in the present is essential to creating more, because then you are grateful for what you have now.

## Live in Your True Essence

Living in your true essence is when you take ownership of what you were meant to do and you live to fulfill it. When you don't live in your true essence and utilize your gifts, you give other people your power.

My intention is to leave a positive impact on everyone, and I need to do it authentically. If someone is having a bad day, what can I do to shift it? Instead of being mean or angry at them in return, how can I shift my energy? Am I honoring my virtue or am I taking what they say personally and letting them have power over me? Embrace your power, embrace your gifts, and utilize them every single day.

Our role in this life isn't to have the biggest house or the biggest and best car. Instead, our purpose is to utilize our gifts. We are handed these gifts for a reason. We need to embrace them in each and every opportunity we have, which is practically every second of the day. What I do believe is that if we utilize the gifts we were born with, those gifts come easily and effortlessly. Everything aligns to make them happen.

# Bonus Chapter: Business Building Secrets

To be self-employed is truly a blessing. What an opportunity it is for us to do something we truly love and to make money doing it. Whether you are a coach, a counselor, or anything else that you love, having a business and doing something you are passionate about is an incredible journey. Some people may get into business to make money, but if you focus more on doing what you love, the money just comes. Remember, you are always taken care of.

If you don't love what you are doing, go do something else. Life is too short to not love what you are doing and to not love your life. If you aren't loving your work, ask yourself, "What's my core purpose in this world? What are my gifts? How can I utilize them?" Even if that means volunteering at first and doing it while you're working at a job, get out there and start doing something you are passionate about. If you are truly doing what you love, the money will come.

## Planting Seeds

When I think of building my business, I call it planting seeds. Planting seeds is about building connections, creating referrals, and generating business through word of mouth. Some other people call this prospecting.

I love receiving referrals, because I'm already sold. All I have to do is walk in and list the house. Many people focus on getting business from strangers, but I learned straight from the gate that working through referrals was the way I wanted to build my business. In real estate they tell you to "farm a neighborhood." That means doing things like sending out "Just Listed" postcards to 100 of the neighbors to share with them what's going on in the market or knocking on doors to pick up clients. But when you do this, you are spending your time, money, and energy on strangers.

Right now in business, it's more important to have a relationship and some kind of connection with people. I believe the next ten years of income for people will be generated through the power of connection. That could mean something as simple as when you look for office supplies, you use a person you previously met at a networking event instead of hitting the local office supply store. People are still spending money in our current economy, but they are spending money with people who matter and with people who are important to them.

We are in the technology age. It's the biggest technology stage in the history of the world, and it's only going to get bigger. Pretty soon my iPhone will clone me! With that comes a greater desire for high touch, meaning handwritten notes and a personal phone call. Many people use a company called SendOutCards, but neither the sender nor anyone else actually physically touches the card. It was entered on the computer, printed on a machine, and never touched by a human. Have you ever noticed that when you get a handwritten note in the mail, it's the first envelope you open? I've mentioned before that I send out handwritten Christmas cards every year. It takes about fifty hours of my time. I handwrite every single one of them, and hand sign each, then I use a sponge to seal them. I love the process, and I know those who receive my cards love getting them too. They can feel the love I've put into each card.

One client recently told me she used me as her realtor because for the previous ten years I had sent her a birthday card. I hadn't even been in the business ten years earlier, but I had still taken the time to send her a handwritten card. Since I did it consistently each year, she knew that was how I'd take care of her as a client. She understood that I'd make her a priority.

Often, people will close a deal in their business, like when a client buys a car or orders business supplies from a vendor, and the person never hears from their salesperson again. When you truly bring value to your clients, you want to keep in touch with them. Keeping in touch is a way to show them how much you truly appreciate them.

That's what is important. Every day I make twenty-five phone calls and create five handwritten notes. I've done that consistently every single day for the last seven years. Sometimes I might get behind on my cards, but I always do them. Once I had to send forty out at one time, and over the following few days, I received messages and calls back about how much those notes meant to people. Some people only email their clients, but because I get 150 emails a day, I know how easy it is to skip over emails unless they're personally addressed to you. Take the time to write notes and make phone calls, because they and the people you send them to are worth it. People will remember you for it.

The reason you want to make all these phone calls and write all these handwritten notes is to plant those seeds. You want to be in front of people so they remember you and what you do. My friend Angel Tuccy, who wrote *Lists that Saved My Business*, believes you need to have thirty touches before someone becomes a client. Touches are what I just mentioned—handwritten notes, phone calls, invites, thank you notes, face-to-face meetings. When she came to my women's group and talked about this, a couple of gals asked me if that was really true and if I believed it. In my business, I know it takes about fifteen touches. The women were blown away by that because it seemed like a lot. Most people give up after the third contact. If they contact someone and then don't hear back after one or two attempts, people usually give up.

Statistically speaking, 90% of business doesn't even happen until after the fifth contact. Most people give up before they get a chance to get the business. Consistency is key to having a successful business. My friend Trinity would agree. My consistency changed both of our businesses. I called her and followed up over and over again. I never gave up on her. Because of that persistence, she has handed me two deals that closed this past year. I also gave her the one deal I mentioned earlier that generated $12,000 in income for her, and she is extremely grateful that I never gave up on her. Imagine how differently things would have turned out if I hadn't contacted her the fifth or sixth time!

When I started my career, I went to networking groups to meet people. I quickly realized people were out there networking in a way that didn't resonate with me. The hosts were all about themselves, the guest speakers would vomit their business on everyone, and it just left an icky feeling inside of me. I'd walk away with fifty business cards, and pretty soon I had hundreds of cards in my possession but didn't know anyone.

When my database got to about 1,500 contacts, I decided to start a very low-key happy hour networking event on the last Thursday of every month at a local restaurant, Baker Street. That event has been a huge success. I've generated many connections from that one group.

**If you don't host your own event, go to another event and invite all your friends. When you bring more people along it creates abundance for everyone.**

I have the most amazing people walk into my life at my events. They've either come as a guest, or because we were friends on Facebook, or because I personally invited them. The Baker Street event has been such a huge success that a friend mentioned it to the local real estate board, which is part of the reason I was appointed chairman of that organization. When that happened, I realized I wanted to combine my two networks. Although Baker Street has been a huge success for the last four years, it was time to step it up a notch. I realized that if I combined my two networks, the event would be more powerful for everyone. We had our kickoff event and 150 people attended. I'm grateful that I had the courage to bring them together. Hosting those events puts me in front of this large group of people and gives me the opportunity for some great follow-up and the chance to build wonderful relationships.

## Be a Connector & Plant Even More Seeds

When you are a connector, you plant seeds for future business. When you meet someone, even if you don't need or use the products they offer, find other people for them who do want or need their services. For example, I don't cook, but when I meet someone in Pampered Chef, a cookware company, I think about who does love to cook and who would like those products. I don't say to that person, "I don't need any of your products, because I don't cook." If I did, I would have just shot that person down. Why would they use me some day for their house if that's how I treated them and their business? It's way bigger than that. Instead, I ask myself, "Who I do know who loves to cook? Who do I know who would love Pampered Chef? Let me connect them with her." It's bigger than we can even imagine. Even if you don't want something, you may know 100 other people who do. As a result of this practice, I was able to help my friend Mandy, a Pampered Chef representative, generate $15,000 income in one year!

As I mentioned in the previous section, to gain new business I was told to farm neighborhoods, send out postcards, knock on doors in order to connect with more people. It took a lot of time, money, and energy. *Why am I spending time, money, and energy on people who don't even know me*? I wondered. *You've got to win them over, but they don't know you.* What I realized is that it's all about self-worth, meaning that if someone doesn't think they bring enough value, it may seem easier to convince a stranger of one's so-called value than someone who already knows you. *But is it really easier*? I questioned. *And if I do believe in myself and my value, wouldn't it make more sense to focus on those I know*? *Why don't I spend time money and energy on the people who already love me*? *Then, I don't have to start from scratch. Instead, these people already know what I do and they already care about me. I can show them how they can help me by being in front of them, talking about what I specialize in, and inviting them to events.* It's the natural law of reciprocity—when you give to someone else they want to give back.

Instead of having a website or paying hundreds of dollars a month to buy leads, I spent that money on taking my girlfriends to lunch. I tell this to everyone in every industry. People say, "Doesn't that get expensive?" Well, the cool thing is, when you take people to lunch, other people take you to lunch. What you give, you receive. Have you ever gone to lunch with a friend and you offer to pay the bill? Then, they tell you they'll get it the next time. So, schedule the next time. At those lunch meetings, I buy lunch maybe 50% of the time, the other half of the time, people buy lunch for me. It didn't cost me anything more than if I had been eating by myself every day.

Another reason why people ask about the money it costs to take people to lunch is that they are coming from scarcity. It takes money to invest in your business. When you first get started in business, if you don't have any money to take people out, then invite people over to your place and make them lunch or tea.

I decided in my business that every single day, Monday through Friday—if at all possible—I'd schedule a lunch appointment with someone. There are two reasons for this. One reason is that we can get really caught up in being self-employed. Sometimes we forget to clock in and clock out. *Oh my, I never had lunch today, no wonder I'm grumpy.* Do it for your health and well-being. The second reason is to make connections during that hour. You are going to eat anyway, so you might as well eat with someone else. No matter how busy we get, there are still seven lunches, seven dinners, and seven opportunities for coffee we can take to enjoy time with someone else each week.

People don't care about how much you know until they know how much you care. When you spend time with people by having lunch with them, or coffee, or a one-on-one, it shows them how much you care. But, be sure you truly show them you care. There's nothing worse than meeting someone for coffee and in the first few moments, they're pulling out their iPad to show you their portfolio. *Seriously*? It's such a big turnoff. It's like foreplay. If you are at a networking event and some-one shows you their portfolio of all the remodeling jobs they've done, it's like, *Wait a minute! I just met you and we haven't even had coffee yet, and you are going for the goal. Let's at least have lunch first, before you go there.*

So many people vomit their business all over every-one else. Generally speaking, it's a big turnoff for most people. No one wants to feel like they're being sold to. At my listing appointments or at coffee appointments, these are the words I say, "So, tell me how I can help you." It's amazing what happens next. They might say a few things that could help them or they might answer that even having lunch together has helped them. Or maybe they express that they need to sell their car or are looking for a carpet cleaner. It's a powerful thing to ask, "How can I help you?"

In the process of mentoring another real estate agent, I showed her how I run my business. We had a lunch scheduled with a lender and she was coming along to observe. As the lender talked, I was 100% pres-ent with him. He then said, "I've been talking a lot Faith. What about you?"

I replied, "I love helping people, so tell me how I can help you."

"Wow, I've been in this business fifteen years and

no one has ever asked me that!" He paused and then was quite articulate about the ways I could help him. By the time he left, an hour-and-a-half later, he said he felt on top of the world. The gal I was mentoring was blown away. He was a lender and I am a real estate agent! He knew what I did, that I was a realtor, but if I was able to make him feel like he was on top of the world, I was sure he would want to send me business. He might not even know why, but he will. And the agent I was mentoring in the real estate business went on to win an award for being one of the top-producing agents at the local real estate board. I must be doing something right!

## See Your Value & the Power of Connection

The number one reason people don't make phone calls is that people don't believe they are bringing enough value to the table. In my world, I believe I bring a lot of value—whether it's connecting someone to an insurance gal who can save them $400 a year on their insurance or helping them buy or sell a property. I find that I cannot even possibly make enough phone calls in a day because that's how much value I bring.

One of the women in my women's group is an energy auditor. She does energy audits for Xcel Energy. She was the 350th person on that list, pretty much at the bottom of all the other auditors. I also knew another person who was on that list—a man who was listed as Number 10—so I thought they should meet. "Maybe you guys can be power partners in some way," I told each of them. It turned out that the guy in tenth position needed an energy auditor who spoke Spanish. He'd been turning down clients because they needed someone who was Spanish-speaking and he wasn't. It turned out my friend is fluent in Spanish. Through that introduction, he realized that working with her could open up a section of the business he'd been turning away. They hired her part-time and it generated $35,000 in income for her. If I hadn't thought outside the box (why would someone want to introduce two people to each other who do the same thing?), if I hadn't believed there was enough value for me to connect these two individuals, then they might not have ever found each other.

People underestimate the power of connection. Because it's something I do naturally, I feel the power of possible connections intuitively and intentionally. I pay attention to those impulses and inklings. I've told the Universe that I'm listening, and because I do, I keep getting more. When we don't listen, we miss opportunities. The key is to listen and take action based on those intuitive "hits" without worrying about the hows or whys.

Do you think my friend is going to use me if she needs to buy or sell a house? You betcha! She even sent me a listing referral—her landlord. When you give without expectations, whether in business or personally, and you connect someone with something or someone else they need, they'll remember you for it. The power of connection is instrumental to receiving more in your life, because people want to give back. My New Year's resolution this year was to spend more time with the givers. Givers give and takers will keep on taking.

Speaking of taking, you might have clients who just

take, take, take. You might be making some money off of it, but in the long run it might not be worth the money if they are sucking your energy dry. Spend time with people who are givers, because they will naturally want to give back. People who are takers are stuck in entitlement. They believe they are owed something.

An agent I know literally thought he was entitled to his entire family's real estate listings. I asked him what he was going to get his grandmother as a closing gift, and his reply was "Nothing. It's the least she owes me." Needless to say, he's no longer in the business. If you treat people like that, it will come back to you, and other people will treat you the same way.

Your past clients are your number one fans. But how often do people really keep in touch with their past clients? They might send them a Christmas card...maybe. You should visit your past clients every other month. Check in with them. *How is your house*? *How's the yard now that it's spring*? That will go a lot further than having a meeting with a stranger you just met. Call and talk to people about the little things. Check in with them. When you stay in touch with people, they'll want to give back to you.

One thing I tell people is to show up at your friend's or past client's house and surprise them with homemade cookies. Don't you think you will win them over again and again? Instead of putting up open house signs and knocking on strangers doors, do something personal for someone. Who opens the door when they aren't expecting someone or don't know who is on the other side? Why not bake cookies and bring them to your past clients and your number one fans?

I was with my girlfriend Nichole and another woman at dinner recently. I commented to the other girl that Nichole was one of my biggest raving fans. Nichole said, "You got that right! You are good at what you do." Do you think that's the girl I should take to dinner? Heck, yeah! I'm going to buy her flowers on her birthday and do anything I can for her. Those things will go so much further because she already believes in me. It's much more powerful than trying to talk to a stranger, or buying leads, or having a big fancy website to attract new clients.

Give gratitude to those you appreciate and who appreciate you. If you cooked dinner for someone every night and they never appreciated it or said thank you, one day you would stop cooking dinner for them. The same goes for referrals. Give appreciation to the people who continue to send you referrals. If you truly believe in the value you are bringing to everyone, you will make those phone calls, send those thank you cards, and call those past clients to see how their new house is working out for them.

It reminds me of the scene in *Pretty Woman*, when she's dressed like a hooker and she's got all that cash to spend. The women in the store judge her and look at her as if to say, "Who are you?" Then, she goes to the next shop and walks out with $10,000 worth of clothes. She returns to the first shop and matter-of-factly states, "Big mistake, BIG!" That's how I feel about people who don't appreciate their current and past clients. It's a big mistake. The number one way to bring more into your life is to be appreciative for what you already have.

Know where your business comes from. Look at the current business you have or the past business you've had and see where it originated. Seventy-five percent of my business comes from referrals. So I spend 75% of my time, energy, and money on people who already love me. The other 25% comes from floor (a way to pick up clients from call-ins to the office) or sign calls (when someone calls me from one of my current listings), so I spend the other 25% of my time working on those other tools that bring me business.

If you bring enough value and show people your value, you shouldn't have to ask for the business. I truly believe that.

## Mathematical Equation to Business

In all of business, there's a mathematical equation. I like sharing the equation for the people who are worried about the how. It's a good way for them to have something tangible to hold on to. I know if I make twenty-five phone calls a day, I will generate ten appointments a week, which will generate one closing every two weeks, or twenty-five closings for the year. Mathematically, I want to have fifty-two closings this year, so if I go back to my equation for how my business works, I need to make fifty phone calls a day and get twenty appointments a week, which will give me four closings per month.

Even if you are new in your business, if you've had three clients buy from you, look at how many calls, how many emails, how many face-to-face meetings it took to get those three closed transactions. It all refers back to little steps. It's the "slight edge" effect. Doing the same thing consistently every single day will create a compound effect in your business. Writing five handwritten cards a day has definitely reaped its rewards in my business.

If you ate a Big Mac today, would it make a difference in your life? Probably not. But what if you ate one every single day, would that impact your health? Definitely. The slight edge is taking something you do every single day and making a huge result out of it. Break it down daily and do it consistently.

If you need three appointments a week, know what it takes to get those appointments. Once you figure out your equation then it's easier to duplicate it.

## Do the Things You Love

In real estate, I am great at open houses. I worked retail for ten years, so I have a lot of experience working with people who are just walking into someplace. I say, just give me a warm body. I love doing open houses. I could do open houses all day long. But if *you* don't love doing open houses, don't do them. Find another way to do business. Maybe farming is better. Maybe social media is better for you. Find a portal that you are good at and do that. The cool thing is that 75% of my business comes from referrals, and I don't even do open houses anymore.

When you are self-employed, you might have to do other tasks that you maybe aren't so good at. Hire someone else to do those things. My friend Nichole Walker says, "Do your best; outsource the rest." One of the best things I did for myself was hire a short-sale specialist. It was about five years ago when I did that. I had to negotiate the deals with the bank and it was heartbreaking when they didn't work out. When I lost a $38,000 paycheck, I said that from then on someone else could call the bank. I'll do what I do best, which is getting the listings and getting them sold. It was the best thing I did for my business.

The second best thing I did was hire my personal assistant. The reason I chose the assistant I have now is because she has the strengths I don't. She is organized, which is a skill set I needed. She didn't know the real estate business when I hired her, but I do. It's perfect harmony. If you are self-employed, hire people who are good at what they do and allow yourself to be good at what you do. Instead of trying to do everything yourself, it's just good business sense.

I have found that a lot of businesses won't hire an assistant because they come from scarcity. They are afraid that they won't have the money to pay for them, even if they're currently busy and making money. But, what if that assistant could bring you more business and you could hire another person? Plan your business so that the person can bring you income. It's one of the best things you can do for your business. With an assistant, what if you only had to work twenty hours instead of forty hours to make the same amount of money? Work smart, not hard.

## The Little Things

Follow-up is absolutely essential for a successful business. If you don't have good follow-up, learn to do it. Have your calendar set to go off to remind you of what you need to do. If you are with someone interested in meeting with you, schedule it right then and there. If any person shows any kind of buying signal, make sure you follow up with them. If you don't, someone else will.

The same goes with consistency. Do the same thing all the time with every client. That means being on time and being prepared, every single time you show up with a client.

If you have a client, don't cancel a previously scheduled commitment to spend time with that client. Pretty soon, if you've cancelled all your coffees and lunches and networking events, you won't have any new clients flowing to you. Remember to not bite off the hand—or hands—that feed you. Keep in mind that when anyone feels the need to jump on a potential client, they're most likely operating from a scarcity mentality, feeling afraid that nothing else will come their way. Yet, when we operate from abundance, and continue to cultivate and nurture our existing relationships, more will always come our way. When you plant enough seeds, you always have more than enough blooming!

One of my pet peeves is when people don't show up to networking events because they have a client. *You* scheduled a client during the meeting time that had already been on your calendar—those networking events are usually scheduled out way in advance. And the reason you have those clients is because you come to those meetings. I suggest that people tell their client (or potential client), "I have a standing appointment from 2:00 to 4:00 p.m., but I can meet you before or after or on another day this week." Nine out of ten times they are going to say okay. They respect you more when you show them your boundaries.

## Setting Your Schedule

I make my phone calls in between my appointments because I need to be flexible in my business. I'm always driving back and forth to show properties. Some people will make excuses and say they can't drive and talk and take notes. But if you are driving and talking, just ask that person to text you the information if you need to write it down and can't right then. Later, you can do what you need to do. You can also make phone calls if you arrive to a place early or when someone else is late. Take a minute or two to make those phone calls when you have free moments. If you need a set schedule for making those calls, do that instead.

To know who to call, I put my clients into a category: A, B, and C. Then I work through my A list first, my B list next, and my C list last. Call the people who are most important to you first. You'll get through those calls quickly. Then, call people you haven't talked to in thirty days. Some may say that they're not ready to buy, but they might be the following month. So, then ask them if you can call them back the next month and pick a date. You'll quickly have people who are ready for you to call because you put them down in your calendar. And you'll never run out of people to call either.

Another practice that is really divine and simple is to ask, "Who should I call right now?" When I ask, the answers always appear. People get caught up on who to call. Who cares? Call your mom. Call me. "Faith, I'm starting my twenty-five calls and I thought I would call you first." "Awesome," I'll tell you. "Thank you for calling."

People will spend an hour-and-a-half deciding who to call, but that's bull. If you are spending that much time on who to call it's because you don't think you are bringing enough value. You don't want to bother people or act like a solicitor. I'm not calling people to ask them to buy or sell a house. I'm calling them to wish them a happy holiday, to invite them to my networking event, or to see how I can help them.

When someone on those calls asks me "How are things?" I say I'm blessed. Then, I ask them, "How can I help you?" I ask them about their business. If they ask you about yours, they are inviting you to talk about it. I ask if they want to know what's going on in their neighborhood or offer something else to help them with their house. It also helps to find commonalities with people. I have a puppy, so I always ask people about their pets. It's about building a relationship instead of selling them.

People also spend a lot of time on non-income producing activities. Sending out mass emails isn't really generating new business. Do stuff that is money generating. Do the twenty-five calls because they will generate money. People tend to get caught up in the busy work. When you have a client, there is stuff you need to do that makes sense. No matter how busy I get I spend two hours a day prospecting. It's the way to get off the rollercoaster—you know, the times when you have clients and then you don't have clients. I consider a lot of activities prospecting—two coffee meetings for one hour each can be my two hours of prospecting. Networking or parties, or whatever it takes to get where you want to be in your business—spend your time doing things that bring in business.

## Connection, Connection, Connection

Remember, connection is the key to growing your business. More than 50% of searches for businesses are being done on Facebook instead of Google. Why? Because Facebook is all about connection. If someone is going to look for a realtor, they are going to go on Facebook and ask their friends who they recommend rather than Google "Realtor Colorado." People want to work with someone they know. Use your network and your connections—plant those seeds. Write notes to people, have face-to-face meetings, and nurture those seeds so that one day they will bloom.

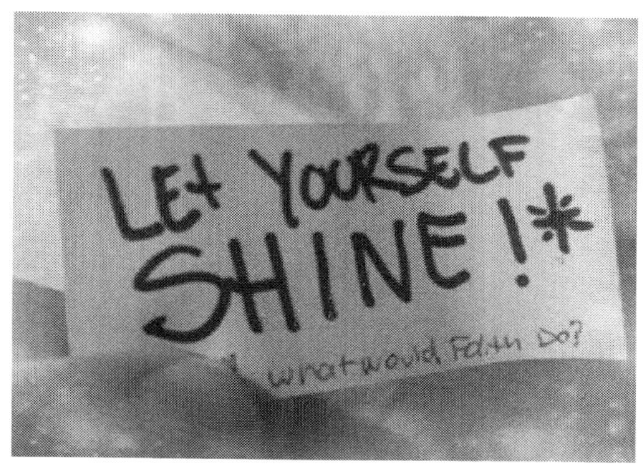


# Epilogue: An Ounce of Faith – One Man's Story

My friend, Don Jackson, went from making $0 to $200,000 per year in twelve months. Unemployed, living in the room of a friend's house, with no working car, he had lost all sense of himself—his self-worth. All of us can relate to that feeling, I'm sure, but I do believe that men especially tend to lose their self-worth and identity with the loss of their job.

We began to talk regularly, and with my coaching, he started to see and feel my belief in him as well as my belief in the possibilities that something better was on its way. As a result, he began to see the possibilities for himself.

When he surrendered and stopped trying to control

when, how, and where (the outcome) his next job would come about, something amazing happened. Within five hours of our conversation, when he released his need to have everything go a certain way, he received in his email inbox the offer of an interview.

Don was extremely excited about the interview. At the moment he read the email, he owned the possibility of what could happen from there. He then saw that not only could he earn $95 an hour (he knew that was the pay for the position), but he was able to hear me say, "What if you could earn another $10 an hour?" Entertaining that question created space for something more to happen. By opening his mind to the possibility of $10 more per hour, he actually received a hiring bonus of $10,000, which set him up to earn $110,000 for the year. Twelve months later, another company came to him and presented an opportunity for him to do the same job with less travel. Even more exciting, he was offered that job with a salary of $200,000.

Now, not only is he making $200,000 per year, but he's driving the car he's always wanted to drive and he's engaged to be married. Everything has aligned perfectly for Don, all because he began to believe in himself and the possibility that something better could and would happen in his life. I believed in Don so much that I gave him the spark and the ounce of faith to believe in himself.

Everyone has a light inside. We were all born with that light. But for most of us, somewhere along the way, it got put out—it was extinguished. I like to be the spark in people's lives to help you reignite your flame. Just like Don, with belief in yourself and in the possibility of what your life can become, you truly can be the shining light you were always meant to be.

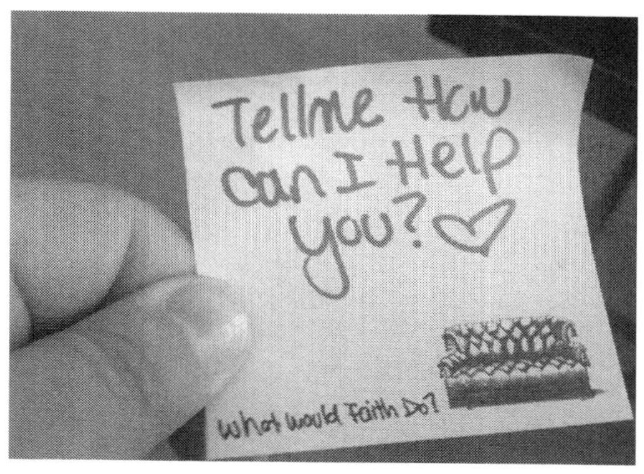


# Faith's 10 Tips for Success

1. Follow up with everyone.
2. Be accountable and dependable to everyone.
3. Consistency in action—consistently is results. Choose actions that you commit to and do them consistently.
4. Relationships—never see anyone as instant gratification. Focus on the long-term relationships. Don't waste time or money on total strangers. Instead, build the relationship.
5. Utilize the natural law of reciprocity—give to others and they will give to you. Not equal value; it's equal commitment. Give referrals without expectations.
6. Connect personally with people. Offer value to

others without any expectations. Call them consistently.

7. Establish your work ethic based on your productive times and keep yourself accountable.
8. Focus your networking and connecting to determine your power partners.
9. Ask your friends to connect you to their number one fan.
10. Let people get to know you first. Don't sell your product/business first. Show them who you are by showing how much you care. Always ask, "How can I help you?"

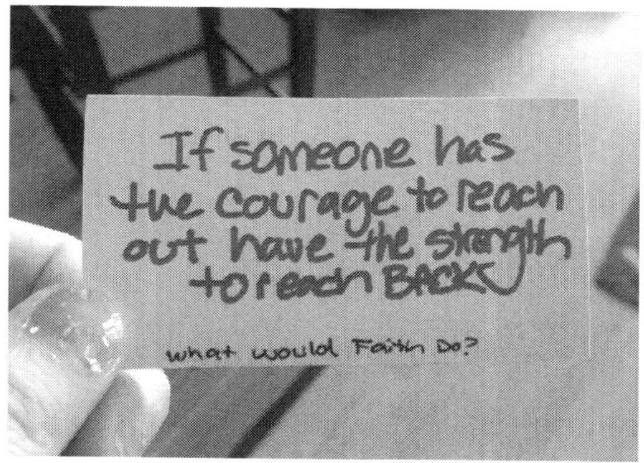


# Faithisms

- Don't beat myself up for yesterday, just learn from it.
- It's bigger than I could imagine.
- It's bigger than this right now!
- I have more than enough time for people who are important to me.
- I make such a powerful shift in myself that it makes other people shift around me.
- My intention is to release any hidden belief that no longer serves me.
- Your wish is my command.
- Don't worry about the how, just believe it's possible.
- I never underestimate the power of the little

things I do each and every day and how they can powerfully impact someone's life!

- That's their sentence, not mine.
- If someone has the courage to reach out, have the strength to reach back!
- Wake up every morning knowing something magical is about to happen!
- *Faith it* til you make it.
- Be the reason people show up.
- Be the gift people are seeking.
- Every good deed I do in this lifetime sets me up for success in the next.
- When I utilize my gifts, everything in the Universe rearranges so that I can share my gifts and talents easily and effortlessly.
- When I get in alignment with what I was meant to do, things just start to line up.
- When I am listening, the answers will appear.
- Each and every day, I recharge my batteries.
- I am open, willing, and able to receive.
- If my cup is half full, how can I fill up someone else's? I take time each and every day to fill up my cup!
- I have the courage to ask, "What can I do to help?"
- I believe all things are made possible by the power of FAITH!
- The best way to attract more into my life is by being grateful for what I have NOW!
- What I think about I bring about.
- People serve a purpose in my life. Sometimes we

make such a powerful shift, we no longer serve each other.

- The best way to teach someone something is to lead by example.
- I am the gift I have been seeking.
- We can all shine on a good day, but how you show up on a bad day shows your true colors.

# Acknowledgments

There are many people to thank in helping me get *What Would Faith Do* out into the world. First, to my mother and father for bringing me into this world, and to my yoga teacher for giving me the name for my book. To my friend, Brian Vatwer, for being a part of my MacBook story and for believing in me. To Trey Malicoat, my life coach, who inspired me to think bigger and who worked with me on ideas for this book. To Greg Mooers, who witnessed and helped me to step into my power to become who I am meant to be. To Andrea Costantine and Donna Mazzitelli for making this all possible!

I found myself sitting in hospice, where my beautiful friend, Maricela Pepe, would live her last days…and I found myself instinctively asking her, "What can I do for you?" She said so simply, "Love me!" That's all any of us really want, isn't it—to be loved?

Love yourself, love each other, and allow yourself to be loved, always and forever.

# About the Author

## Keynote Speaker, Author, Professional Coach and Trainer

Faith Young lives her life through the power of love. Throughout the course of her life, she has overcome many challenges, including thirteen car accidents, a miscarriage, and a divorce. Through it all, she's had faith and learned how to master the power of positive thinking.

Today, she is passionate about sharing that love with others, spreading empowerment, and giving people the tools they need to live an abundant loving life. She lives by her Heart Virtues, the most important values in her life, which are "empowerment and faith." Faith's purpose in life is to "spread the love" and let people know that she believes in them.

The amazing Faith Young was born and raised in the suburbs of Denver, Colorado. Her challenging life experiences gives her the ability to inspire, guide and empower others through theirs. She is a dynamic speaker, trainer author and lifter of souls. She is one of the top, award winning, realtors in the nation and she serves on the board of the Board of Realtors for the Young Professional Network in Colorado. She lives with her puppy, a five-pound Chihuahua, named Boo Boo.

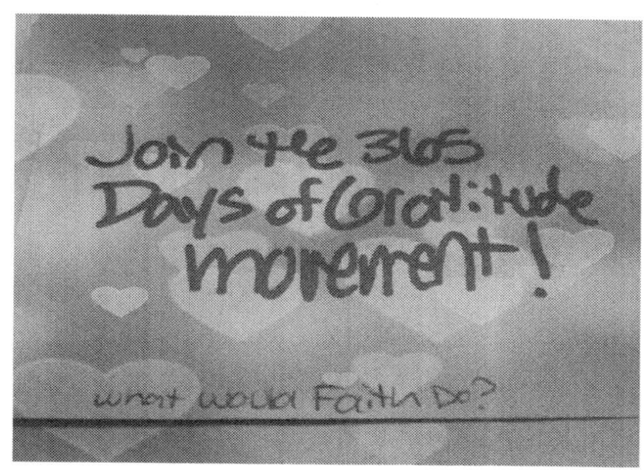


*What Would Faith Do Movement*

My ultimate goal is to have seven billion people know I believe in them. With Facebook, I can access one billion of those people. It's a way to spread the love quickly, effortlessly, and abundantly. I'd love for you to join my movement online at www.WhatWouldFaithDo.com.

Join our Facebook fan page where I share my "What Would Faith Do" notes. Share these posts with your friends and spread the empowerment. Remember, it's not "*What Would Faith Young Do*?" These messages are meant to share the movement. It's about showing people how to spread the love and share it unconditionally. We are all craving love. Whether it's a handwritten note, a face-to-face meeting, or a phone call, people want that *touch* to know that someone cares. Join the movement online now!

Connect with Faith online:
Facebook: www.facebook.com/pages/What-would-Faith-Do/190637767687257

Share your story on the What Would Faith Do? Blog at http://whatwouldfaithdo.com/blog/

Twitter: www.twitter.com/whatwouldfaith

Made in the USA
Charleston, SC
13 October 2013

JAKE
GRAP

# TRICK-SHOT TRIUMPH

STONE ARCH BOOKS
a capstone imprint

Published by Stone Arch Books,
an imprint of Capstone.
1710 Roe Crest Drive
North Mankato, Minnesota 56003
capstonepub.com



Library in Congress Cataloging-in-Publication Data
Names: Maddox, Jake, author. | Garcia, Eduardo, 1970 August 31– artist.
Title: Trick-shot triumph / text by Daniel Mauleón ; art by Eduardo Garcia.
Description: North Mankato, Minnesota : Stone Arch Books, 2022. | Series: Jake Maddox graphic novels | Audience: Ages 8-11 | Audience: Grades 2–3
Summary: Mariana and her new friend, Selena, lose a basketball game to some older girls at a local court but have the confidence to challenge them and win back Selena's special autographed jersey.
Identifiers: LCCN 2021030715 (print) | LCCN 2021030716 (ebook) | ISBN 9781663959133 (hardcover) | ISBN 9781666328448 (paperback) | ISBN 9781666328455 (pdf) | ISBN 9781666328479 (kindle edition)
Subjects: CYAC: Graphic novels. | Basketball--Fiction. | Self-confidence-- Fiction. | LCGFT: Sports comics. | Graphic novels.
Classification: LCC PZ7.7.M332 Tr 2022 (print) | LCC PZ7.7.M332 (ebook) | DDC 741.5/973--dc23
LC record available at https://lccn.loc.gov/2021030715
LC ebook record available at https://lccn.loc.gov/2021030716

Editor: Aaron Sautter
Designer: Brann Garvey
Production Specialist: Laura Manthe

Printed and bound in the USA. PO4608

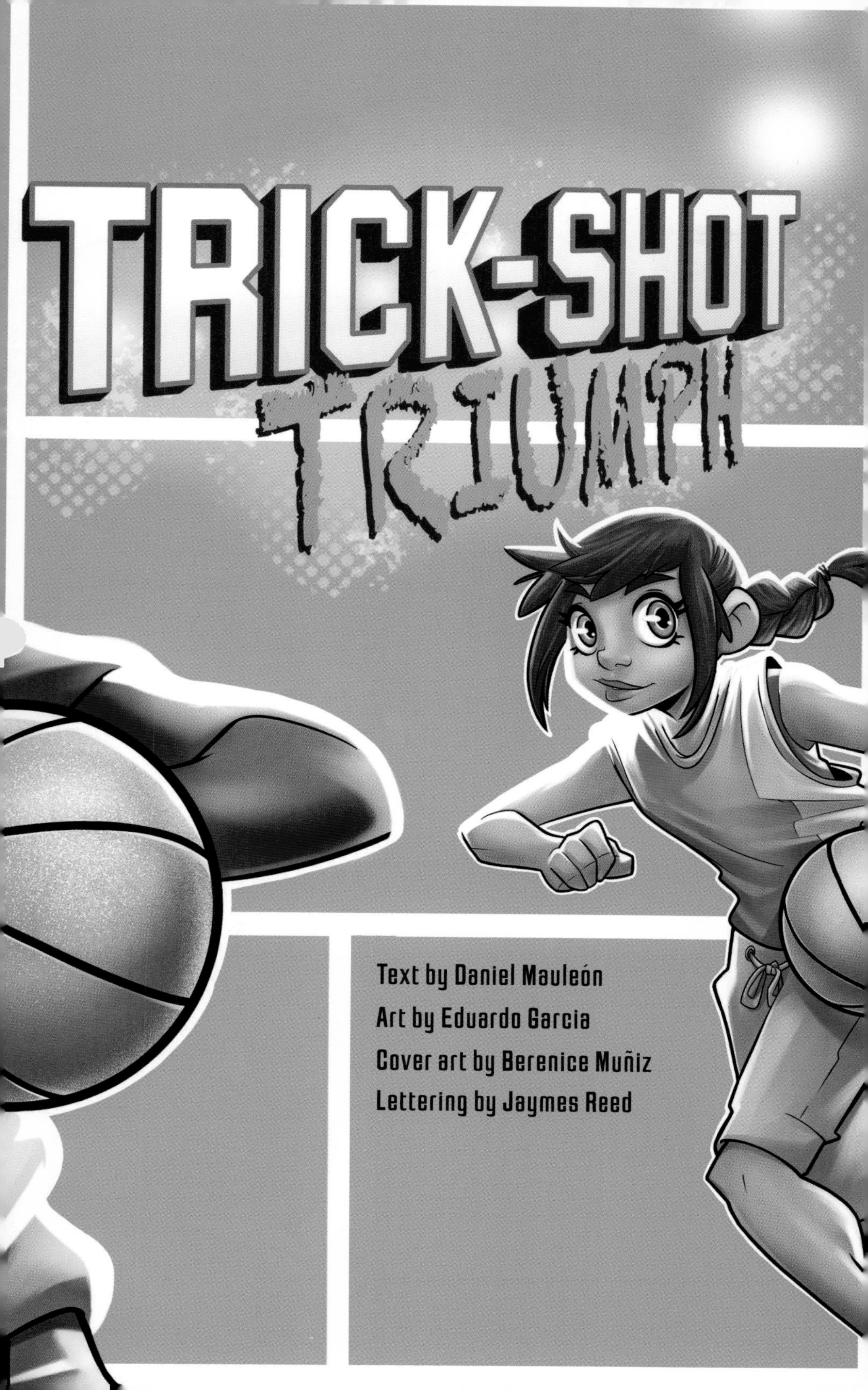

# TRICK-SHOT TRIUMPH

Text by Daniel Mauleón
Art by Eduardo Garcia
Cover art by Berenice Muñiz
Lettering by Jaymes Reed

MARIANA

SELENA

KAT

TINA

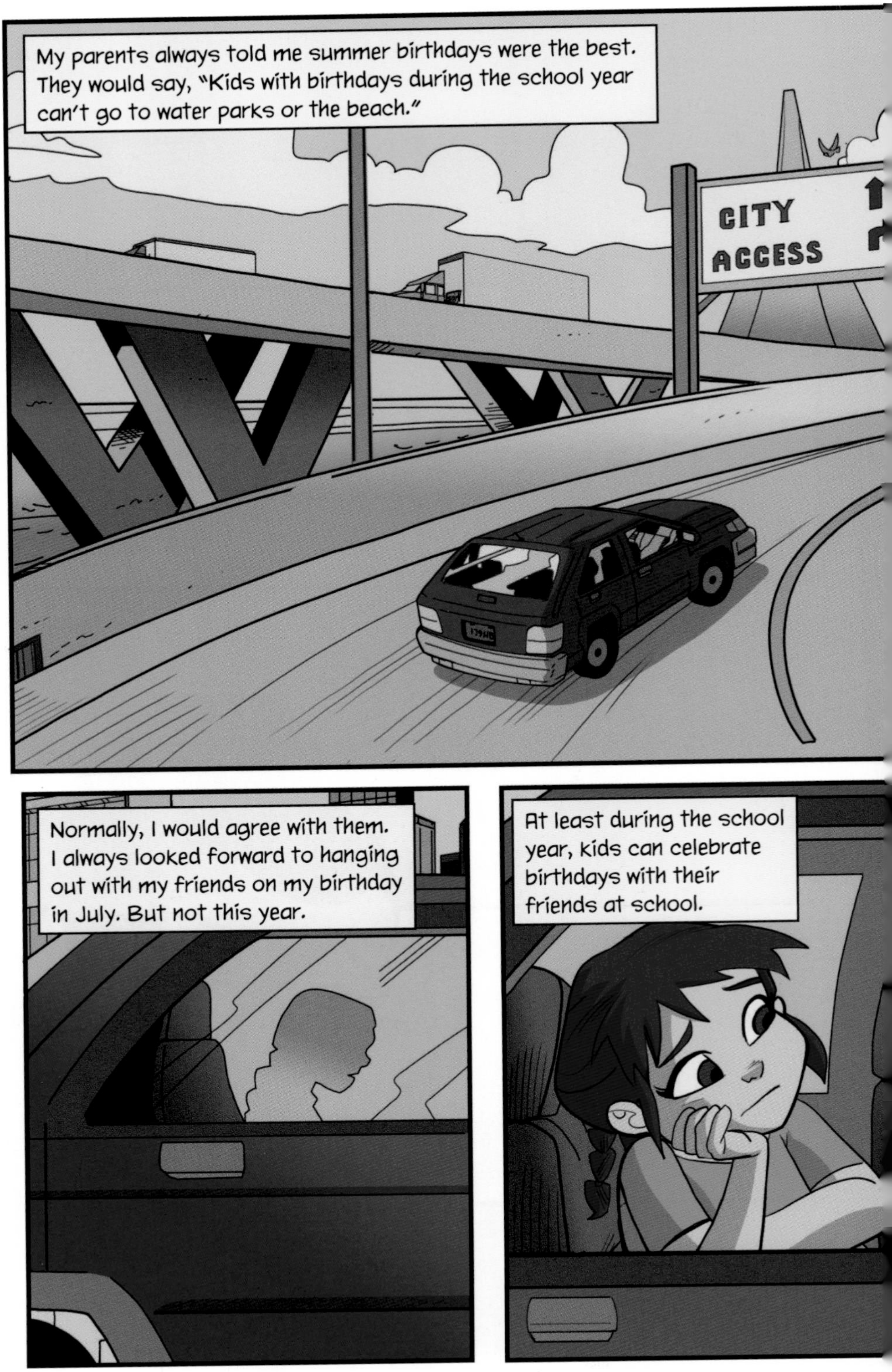

My parents always told me summer birthdays were the best. They would say, "Kids with birthdays during the school year can't go to water parks or the beach."

CITY ACCESS

Normally, I would agree with them. I always looked forward to hanging out with my friends on my birthday in July. But not this year.

At least during the school year, kids can celebrate birthdays with their friends at school.

But what fun is a birthday at the beach or the waterpark when you can't spend the day with your friends?

When you move to a new city on the first day of summer, it's not like you can take your friends with you.

When we pull into the driveway of our new home, all I can think about is my old city, my friends, and how much I was going to miss them.

My parents told me we'd have a neighbor that was my age. They said I'd have a new friend in no time.

But when I saw her playing basketball in her driveway, I knew my parents were wrong. I don't play sports—so this friendship is doomed before it even begins.

I guess I'll just lay low for the summer and catch up on some reading and TV shows. Maybe I'll meet some new kids at school this fall. They can't all like sports in this city.

WATCH OUT!

AAAHHH . . .

. . . hhhhh?

Sorry!

I might not become this girl's friend, but I'm not going to be rude. Even if she did almost hit me with the ball.
I've got it . . . here, catch.
Take a shot!
I don't want to look foolish . . .
. . . but I don't want my new neighbor to think I'm wishy washy either.

To both of our surprise, I nail the shot.

FWIP!

WHOA!

The next morning, I see Selena is out practicing again. She misses more shots than she makes, but she never stops trying. I guess it's one way to spend a day.

As for me, my day looks like an unpacking party.
<sigh>

I guess she *does* do more than play basketball.

DING...
DONG...

I shouldn't be surprised to see who's at the front door.

Hey there. What are you doing today?

Umm . . . unpacking?

Great! Sounds like that can wait, come shoot with me.

I, uh, okay.

Okay, sure. I'm not a big sports fan.

But shooting hoops is better than spending the day unpacking boxes.

That was a great shot you made yesterday.
Have you played before?

Nope. I've never touched a basketball before yesterday.

Seriously? Well, you could have fooled me.
That shot was flawless!
But there's more to basketball than just shooting.

For the next week, Selena shows me the basics of basketball.
The first thing you should learn is dribbling.

Dribbling looks easy. But it's trickier than it seems.

It does look pretty—

BONK!
OUCH!

Passing the ball seems similar to shooting it. I didn't think passing it would be too hard.

I'm open!

Oops.

Yikes!

THONK!

Selena tries hard to teach me, but I'm not great at the other basketball stuff. I have a lot of practicing to do. We did find out one thing though . . .

. . . my shooting skills weren't just beginner's luck.

Between practicing dribbling and passing, Selena and I have shootouts.
SWISH!

The shootouts are pretty fun, and they often turn into trick-shot competitions. I can sink the ball from my driveway . . .
SWISH!

. . . and one time while our parents were out . . .

Did you see that? I made it!

That was insane, Mariana!

I thought it would be hard with the window blocking my view, but . . .

You have to be the best basketball player I know! Personally, I mean. But still . . .

It went in! Oh my gosh. I can never tell my parents. I've been told not to throw things in the house.

And maybe only at shooting. But you'll get the rest in time.

Did I really throw it in the house?

You'll be unstoppable!

I surprised myself. I've never been big on sports. But a week after moving into our new house, I was playing and loving basketball. Plus, I even had a new best friend.

Ugh, I hate rainy days. I'd still play, but my mom tells me I'll get sick.

Thing is, I'd still play even if I *was* sick.

Ha ha! You really love basketball, don't you?

Absolutely! It's an amazing game.
My mom thinks I love it too much.
But I don't care. Hey, I want to show you something!

You won't believe this! Now, where is it?

Aha! Here it is!

That's so cool! Why haven't I seen you wear this before?

23

Oh, this jersey is pretty special.

I got it for my birthday last year. It's even autographed!

I wouldn't want anything bad to happen to it.

23

When's your birthday Mariana?

Well, actually . . . it's in two days.

And you're just telling me *now*? Mariana!

I wasn't trying to keep it secret.
When we moved here I just thought I'd be celebrating by myself.

Are you kidding? We've got to plan a slumber party!
I need to get you a gift!
It's short notice, but I'll make sure you have the best party yet.

I never expected it, but hanging out and shooting hoops with Selena turned out to be one of the best weeks of my life. However, the good times wouldn't last.

The day before my birthday, everything started fine.

Oh my gosh, Selena!

You're wearing it!

Yep! I thought—why have a special jersey and not show it off? You know?
You look amazing!
23

Thanks! I was thinking, there's a park a few blocks from here with an actual court.
Would you want to play there today?
Of course!

Basketball was still new to me, but the way Selena talked about my shooting, I felt I could take on the world!

We're here! You're going to love this place.

DUNK!
Selena was right. There were other girls playing at the court. And they were good.
WOOAAHHH!
That was cool! Do you two want to play?
Ha! No thanks. We don't play with kids.
Can you believe them Kat?
Umm, okay. Then can we use the other half of the court?

Say, that's a
pretty nice jersey.
You know what . . .

Let's play a game after all.

I'm curious if you can beat Tina and me.

First team to 21 wins.

If you two win, you can use the other side of the court.

If we win, we get your jersey.

23

. . . Selena clearly didn't want to do this.
Um, actually . . .


But I had recently found a lot of confidence. Plus, these girls were being bullies. They didn't deserve to hog the court.

Deal. We're gonna wipe the floor with you.

Uh, Mariana . . .

We start the game with the ball. Selena dribbles it past Tina, and then passes it to me. The shorter girl, Kat, is a few feet away. She doesn't think I can make a shot from behind the three-point line.

I want to prove her wrong . . .

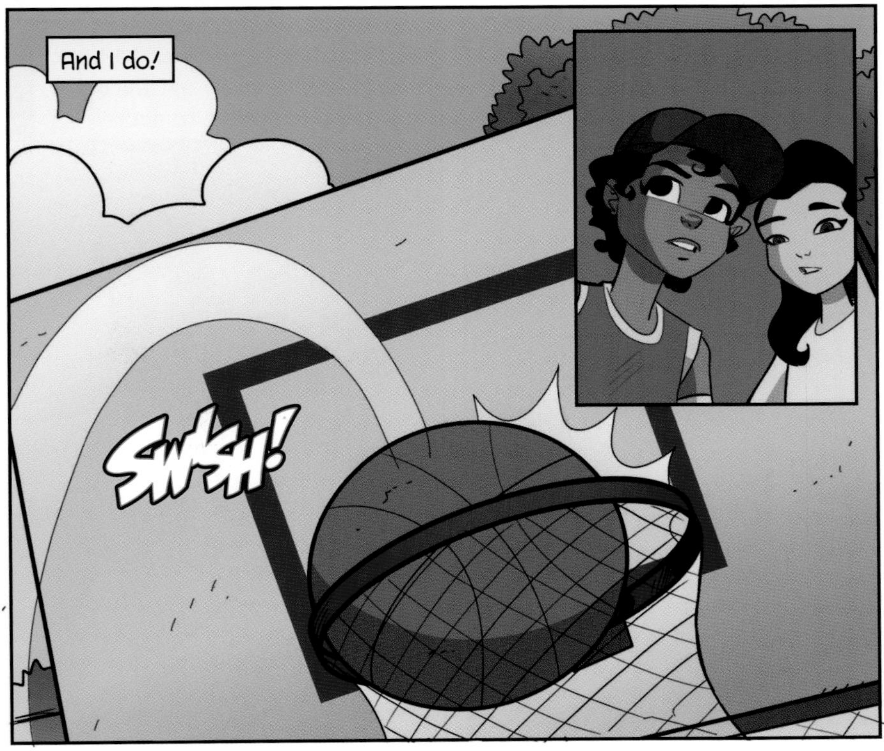

And I do!

SWISH!

Not bad little girl.

Little? You're what?

A year older than me?

I wasn't talking age.

Kat and Tina score back-to-back shots. Then I finally get the ball and another chance to score.

But when I try to take a shot . . .

THUD!

. . . and another . . .
THUD!

. . . and another . . .
THUD!
. . . Kat's defenses are too good. I can't get the ball past her.

They score 17 points before I make another basket.
SCORE: 3-17

Pretty soon my whole game is off. I can't dribble.
OOPS!

Mari! Mari!

I see that Selena is open and has a chance to get to the net. So I try to pass her the ball.

When Kat gets another score off my bad pass, I want to just run away.

SCORE: 5-19

When Kat throws down the final shot, I know I really messed things up.

DUNK!

SCORE: 5-21

You know what? On second thought, y'all can have the court!

HA! HA! HA! HA! HA!

That looks much better on you then it did on her.

I realize that I made a lot of mistakes—and not just in the game.

Selena, I . . . I just thought . . . I, um . . . can you say something?

Selena?

But then I go and make the worst mistake yet . . .

I run away.

How could I have been so selfish? Selena deserves a better friend than me.

I woke up the next day with a pit in my stomach. Two days ago, Selena and I were planning for a slumber party.
Way to ruin your birthday, Mariana.

We were planning a movie marathon. And my parents were going to get us a bunch of snacks.
Then tomorrow we were going to go to the beach.

I really messed things up. Selena told me how special her jersey was. How could I think I was a good enough player to put it on the line? Then I left her there at the court, all alone.

Selena deserves a real friend.

Even if that isn't me . . .

. . . I still owe her an apology.
KNOCK!
KNOCK!
KNOCK!

Oh. Hey.

Selena, I'm so sorry.

I thought I was good enough to win yesterday. But I wasn't.
I took that bet without thinking about what you wanted.
I'm going to save my allowance all summer to buy you a new jersey and—

Hey, stop. You're right.
You shouldn't have made that bet.
But I could have stopped you.
I don't know if I'm ready to forgive you.
But I don't want to be mad at you either.

Thanks.
Well, uh, I guess
I'll be going.
Wait one 
second!

This is
awkward—and
weird. But . . .
it's still your
birthday.


Wow. Selena,
I . . . I don't know
what to say.

Selena is truly a special friend.

I'll do whatever it takes to earn her trust back.

I don't deserve this. Thank you.

Yeah. I thought if you had your own ball you could practice more.

You have a lot of learning to do. We haven't even gotten into layups, stealing, or rebounds yet.

I felt like a huge weight was lifted off of me. The way Selena was talking, I knew we'd be okay.

You'll want to be a well-rounded player for tryouts in the fall.
You're a great shooter.
But in a real game you can't lean on that alone.
Selena's right. I'm not ready for a real game. But maybe . . . 
Hey, Selena, I have a crazy idea.

We should go back to the basketball court . . .
I think I know how to get your jersey back.

When I told Selena my plan, she knew it was risky. But sometimes risks are worth taking.

We get lucky and find Kat and Tina back at the court.

Hey look, the kids are back.

Hope you girls enjoyed your time on the court yesterday.

Because we're not looking to share today.

Actually, I was hoping for a rematch.

Not a two-on-two. Just you and me.

A game of "H-O-R-S-E."

We take turns matching shots around the court.

If you can't make the same shot as me, you—

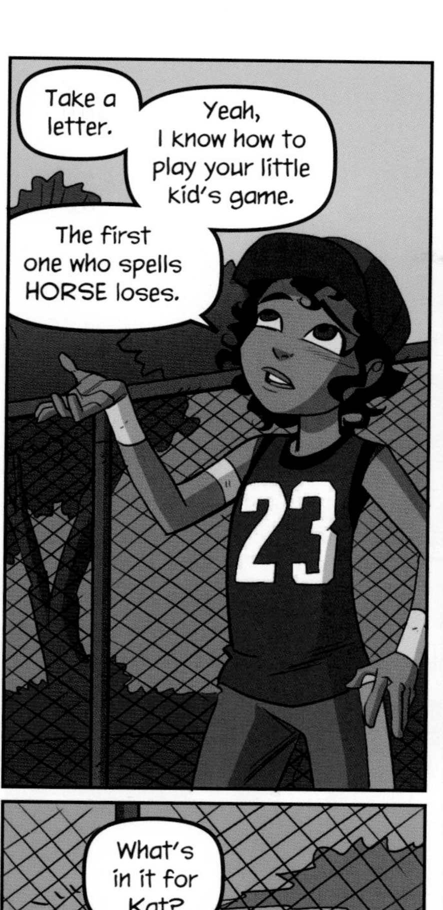
Take a letter.
Yeah, I know how to play your little kid's game.
The first one who spells HORSE loses.
23

Great, I was afraid I'd waste an hour trying to teach you the rules.
So, this is simple.
If I win you give Selena her jersey back.

What's in it for Kat?
23

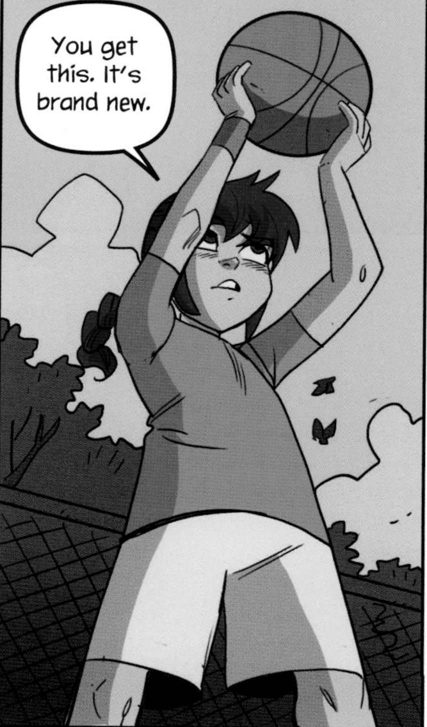
You get this. It's brand new.

Why not?
I mean, you're basically giving it away for free.
23

Deal.
23

You're going to regret this.
If you wanted to win, you should have picked Tina.

SWISH!

I feel worried for a moment. Kat could easily be a better shooter than me. But I take a deep breath . . .
23

23

SWISH!
Hmph! Lucky shot.
Alright! Go Mari!
This is going to be a challenge! But I know I have a real shot to win.
Kat makes an impressive long-range basket.
SWISH!

Unfortunately, I can't match it.
BONK!
That's H for you!
Now it's my turn. I decide to go with something reliable.
Yes!
SWISH!
BONK!
Argh!

After that . . .
SWISH!

. . . we go back and forth. We each take turns trying to make more complicated shots.

SWISH!

THONK!

When Kat slams a dunk, I don't even try to match. I know I can't pull that off.
DUNK!
It's tied up and I'm running out of ideas for shots.
Her height is such a big advantage.
What's your advantage?
23
I can't exactly make a shot from my bedroom window again. However, . . .

Hey, where ya' goin'? Leaving before it's over?

The doorway to the court is pretty low. Maybe if I stand underneath it . . .

SWISH!

Gulp!

As I hoped, Kat's too tall. She has to crouch down awkwardly to avoid throwing the ball into the doorway. Her height is suddenly a disadvantage.

SCORE: HORSE - HORS
YES!
Yes! Mari, you did it!

Ugh, I can't believe I lost to a kid.
Here, take it. Let's go, Tina.

Hey! Wait up a second.

Let's play another round.

No bets. No tricks. One-on-one gets boring, don't you think?
It'd be great if the four of us could just have fun playing a game.

We should mix teams though.
Both of you are way better than us.

I see what she's doing, so I try to help out.
We can play with my new ball.


Selena really is someone special.

Even after my big mistakes, Selena has no problem making new friends. She's the best gift a summer birthday girl in a new city could ask for.

But I'm still going to do my best to beat her in this game!

THE END

# VISUAL DISCUSSION QUESTIONS

1. Establishing shots help set the scene for a story. What can we find out about Mariana's new neighborhood from this panel?

2. Extreme angles are sometimes used to show something important in a story. What can we learn about Mariana's shooting skills from the scene to the right?

**3.** Graphic novels sometimes use a sequence of panels to help tell a story. Study the group of panels to the right. Can you learn anything about Kat's basketball skills from what the art is showing?

**4.** Body posture and facial expressions can often show what people are feeling in the moment. What do you think Mariana and Serena are feeling in these scenes?

# MORE ABOUT BASKETBALL

- Selena's jersey is based on Minnesota Lynx player Maya Moore #23. Moore has won four Women's National Basketball Association (WNBA) championships.

- Additionally, Moore has won two Olympic gold medals playing for Team USA in 2012 and 2016.

- This story features a variety of three-point and half-court shots. In the WNBA, the three-point line is 22 feet, 1.75 inches (6.75 meters) in front of the basket and half-court is more than 45 feet (14 m)!

- Michael "Wild Thing" Wilson, a player for the Harlem Globetrotters, owns the record for highest slam dunk. The hoop was raised to 12 feet (3.7 m), but that didn't stop Wilson!

- During a game in 2002, Allyson Fasnacht made a basket from 81 feet, 7 inches (24.9 m) away. Fasnacht holds the record for the longest field goal by a woman.

# WORK ON YOUR B-BALL SKILLS

## SHOOTING

To win in basketball, you have to score points. And to score points, you have to be good at making shots! Practice making shots from many angles and distances to sharpen your skills.

Good shooting involves more than your arms and hands. Bend your knees, hips, and elbows when preparing to shoot. Then when you take the shot, extend them in that order for a more powerful shot.

## DRIBBLING

Dribbling is a skill every basketball player must know, but it can be tricky to master.

Don't think about dribbling as hitting or knocking the ball. Instead, cup your hand and push the ball down using your fingertips. This gives you better control over the power and direction of the basketball.

When dribbling, keep the ball next to your side rather than in front. This helps in two ways. First, you won't kick the ball as you move up and down the court. And second, it's harder for opponents to steal the ball from across your body.

## PASSING

The best way to keep opponents on their toes is by passing the ball. You won't always have an opportunity to take a shot. But you can help set up your teammates to score with a great pass.

It's often faster to pass the ball a few times up the court than to dribble it to the basket yourself. After passing the ball to a teammate, sprint to your next position. Then get ready to receive a return pass and pass it again if needed.

# GLOSSARY

**advantage** (ad-VAN-tij)—a benefit that someone has over an opponent in a competition

**allowance** (uh-LOU-uhns)—a set amount of money regularly given to someone

**autograph** (AW-tuh-graf)—a person's signature on a piece of paper or other object, often of a famous celebrity or athlete

**competition** (kahm-puh-TI-shuhn)—a contest between two or more people

**confidence** (KON-fi-duhnss)—belief in oneself and one's abilities

**dunk** (DUNK)—when a player jumps and puts the ball directly through the hoop

**marathon** (MAIR-uh-thon)—an event or activity that takes place over a long period of time

**rebound** (REE-bound)—to take possession of the ball after it bounces off the backboard or rim of the basket

**reliable** (ri-LYE-uh-buhl)—trustworthy or dependable

**shootout** (SHOOT-out)—a shooting competition used to determine a winner

# ABOUT THE AUTHOR

**Daniel Mauleón** has never been good at basketball, but over the years he's greatly improved at shooting dirty clothes into a laundry hamper. Daniel graduated from Hamline University with a Masters in Fine Arts for Writing for Children and Young Adults in 2017 and has written a variety of kids' books and graphic novels. He lives with his wife and two cats in Minnesota.

# ABOUT THE ARTISTS

**Eduardo Garcia** works out of Mexico City. He has lent his illustration talents to such varied projects as the Spider-Man Family, Flash Gordon, and Speed Racer. He's currently working on a series of illustrations for an educational publisher while his wife and children look over his shoulder!

**Berenice Muñiz** is a graphic designer and illustrator from Monterrey, Mexico. She has done work for publicity agencies, art exhibitions, and even created her own webcomic. These days, Berenice is devoted to illustrating comics as part of the Graphikslava crew.

**Jaymes Reed** has operated the company Digital-CAPS: Comic Book Lettering since 2003. He has done lettering for many publishers, most notably Avatar Press. He's also the only letterer working with Inception Strategies, an Aboriginal-Australian publisher that develops social comics with public service messages for the Australian government. Jaymes is a 2012 and 2013 Shel Dorf Award Nominee.

# READ THEM ALL!

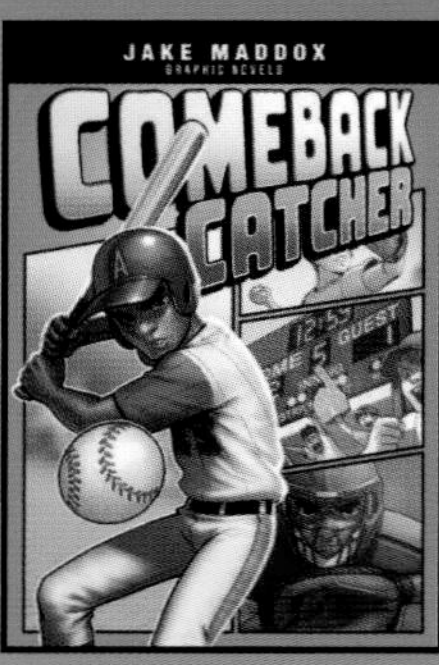

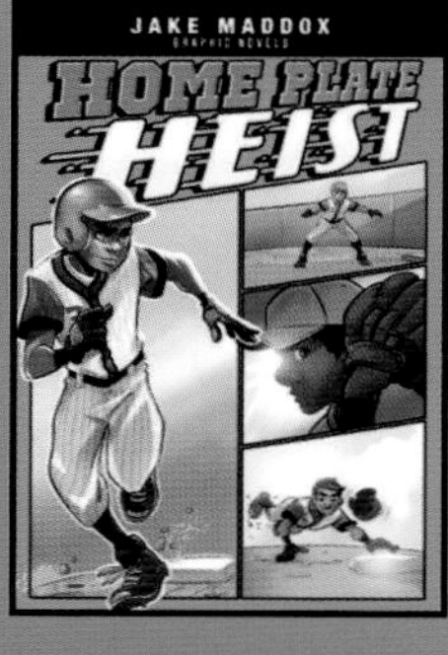

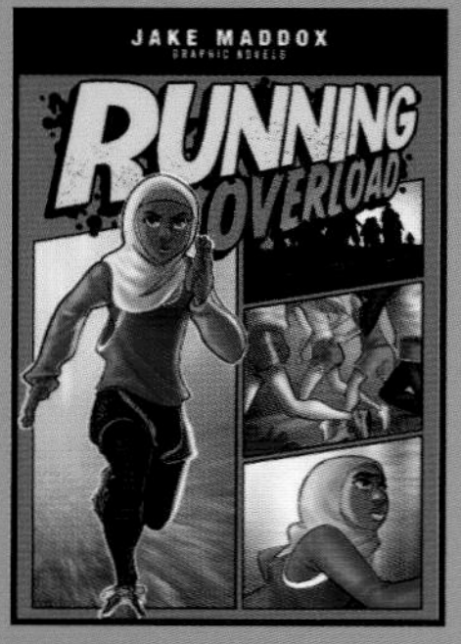

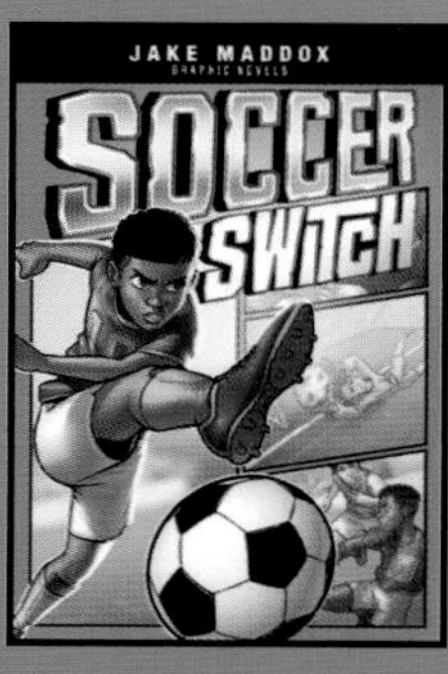